BUILT TO LAST

The Courtship That Leads To A Lasting Marriage

DEREK & SELGELIA AGGREY-SOLOMON

DAS Publishing

Dasolomon@aol.com
Selgelia@yahoo.com

CONTENTS

DEDICATION

This book is dedicated to everyone who is genuinely trusting God to lead them into a happy and lasting marriage. May God's favour locate you, may His wisdom guide you, and may His Spirit help you. Hold on. Press on. It will happen!

ACKNOWLEDGEMENTS

We thank God Almighty for all the grace that He has bestowed on us from a young age. Special thanks to Rev. & Mrs. G. Aggrey-Solomon and Mr. & Mrs. P.D. Quartey, our parents, for the exceptional role models that they are to us and for the sacrifices that they made in ensuring that we were well educated. We honour them for teaching us the way of the LORD from an early age.

We also honour Rev. Dr. Robert Ampiah-Kwofi, Rev. Eastwood Anaba, Rev. Kofi Okyere, Rev. Bob Asare, Bishop Eric Ntorinkansah Rev. Jonathan Ekuban, Mr. & Mrs. John Okine, Mr. W.T. Dziworshie and Pas. Daniel Donkor, anointed and spirit-filled men and women of God, who consciously or otherwise made tremendous impact on our Christian lives. We are ever grateful for Scripture Union, Ghana and Pentefel, University of Cape-Coast, Ghana as they gave us the opportunity to know God better.

Our appreciation also goes to Mrs Diana Alexander for her enormous editorial support.

To our Shine Ministries spiritual family in the United Kingdom and Ghana, we thank you wholeheartedly for believing in our leadership and in standing with us through the years.

FOREWORD

This book is a must read for every person who is even remotely considering marriage as it provides essential information that should be faithfully considered if you are to build a marriage that will last. After marriage, couples discover that their lives have been altered forever and they cannot reverse their course as they are locked in an unalterable path with their partners. Who that partner is, and how he or she was chosen becomes a serious issue. Most couples only discover after marriage how important their partner really is, and how dramatically their partner affects their lives. They realise that their choice of a marriage partner is probably the most important decision they will ever make and it is second only to their decision to accept Jesus Christ as their Lord and Personal Saviour. Many factors that seem important before marriage can become extremely trivial after marriage; beauty is vain and only skin deep, and strong emotions and sexual attractions may fade under the scrutiny of the challenges of married life!

Derek and Selgelia have brilliantly and in a most attractive and easy to read style, set forth principles that will guide you in choosing prospective marriage partners. In a witty and candid manner, they have set out the various courtship principles that they themselves have successfully applied from God's word. Their own love for each other and the great value they place on their relationship is evident in this book, and will encourage couples to emulate their example of Christian courtship.

This book is truly an essential tool that anyone considering marriage must have. Godly principles have been laid out in a systematic manner that provides answers for a multitude of questions that plague the minds of people contemplating marriage. I have personally been acquainted with this couple and can testify to the soundness of their relationship. The principles that have brought them joy and happiness can be yours too, as you study and apply the material in this book in your own search for a suitable mate. God bless you!

Rev. Dr. Robert Ampiah-Kwofi
Global Revival Ministries, Accra, Ghana

INTRODUCTION

There comes a time in the life of a man when he needs a partner. God, after creating man, realised that it was not good for him to be alone. For that reason, he created for man, a woman. This means that a woman is an indispensable partner for a man;a partner so important that man can hardly live without her.

A house can be occupied by anyone but a woman builds a home. It does not matter whether they are housewives or full time professionals. Without a woman, there is no home! Women live all their lives, sorting men out; from finding missing socks to the feeding of a hungry baby. Statistics show that children, who grow up in a home with their mothers, tend to be more intelligent, healthy and mentally stable. Do you know how important breast milk is to the mental and physical development of babies? Women make the world a better place.

Given how important they are, it is desirable for every young man to have one of these precious gems in his life. Sociology tells us that all a man does is aimed at getting the attention and love of a woman and even though the statistics show that there are more women in this world than men, not all men have access to a woman. Ironically, there is also enough evidence that worldwide divorce is on the increase. Research on the other hand also shows that no matter how successful a woman gets in life, she feels inadequate without a man. If these assertions are true, then there is a missing link to the effective organisation of marital relationships and this link can only be found in the word of God. Let us read on and build fortified relationships that lead to impregnable marriages.

CHAPTER 1

THE INITIAL PHILOSOPHY

WHY DO I WANT TO BE IN THIS RELATIONSHIP? – MARRIAGE OR FANTASY

Marriage is a very important institution that often starts with a relationship or courtship. Most courtships also develop from friendships or associations that arise from the proximity that are created by the various institutions of life such as school, the workplace, Church or communal living. As we see and relate with each other, fondness is bound to develop over a period of time. Some attractions also take place at first sight.

There are many devices in a man's heart; nevertheless the counsel of the LORD, that shall stand. – Prov. 19:21

One of the most important questions to ask yourself when you feel drawn to another person is to find out why you want to get close to such a person. Is it just for friendship? Do I want to spend the rest of my life with this person in the commitment of marriage? Or do I just want to use them for fun or the fulfilment of my pleasures or fantasies and move on?

As a Christian, there is nothing wrong with making friends with the opposite sex just for friendship sake but we have to be careful not to allow our hearts to draw us into things that do not please God. It is even more wicked if we have intentions of using people just for our own pleasures. Ask yourself whether your motives are right before you break someone's heart and incur God's displeasure.

You must equally be very careful to discern why others come close to you. Do not be deceived by your beauty or any other attractive qualities that you have. Your heart can be badly damaged by the pain of a broken heart and the regretful feeling of letting yourself down. Take time to get to know people and to see what they really want before you give in to their demands for your love. Certain things, once given away can never be taken back so please take your time.

Take your time to pray well. Take your time to hear from God. Take your time to receive wise counsel. Take your time to make critical observations so as not to have regrets in the future.

Commit thy way unto the LORD; trust also in him; and he shall bring it to pass. – Ps. 37:5

WHY DO I WANT TO GET MARRIED?

Marriage is a honourable thing. It should be everyone's desire to marry but you still have to ask yourself why you want to get married. This is because some of the reasons that drive people into marriage eventually leave them with frustrations and pain. Marriage is great but you must go in with the right motive. That is the only way you can enjoy it.

Why do you want to get married? Is it for sex or companionship? Is it because you are growing old or you need money? Is it because you want to travel or change your social status? Why do you want to get married? Be quite tough on yourself and answer these questions candidly to avoid making painful mistakes.

Search me, O God, and know my heart: try me, and know my thoughts: And see if there be any wicked way in me, and lead me in the way everlasting. – Ps. 139:23-24

AM I UNDER PRESSURE?

Many people marry because of pressure. Pressure from family, pressure from sexual desires, the pressure of their 'body clock ticking' and many other pressures that influence people to just settle for anyone to marry even when it is obvious that they are not compatible, and later they have regrets.

If the foundations be destroyed, what can the righteous do? – Ps. 11:3

The foundation of marriage should be love and nothing else. Once love is not the basis, you are left with emptiness when the associated need is met. Unfortunately, because marriage is for life, you will have to spend the rest of your life with someone you do not love.

THE SEXUAL PRESSURE

Marriage does not cure lust. If you have no control over your sexual feelings, you will still have problems even after you have married. You may have to travel alone, sickness and other situations can arise which may not allow you to have the expected access to sex as envisaged. Of course marriage helps but it is not the all-in-all cure for lack of self-control. So learn how to control yourself and trust God to settle you with the right person.

For if ye live after the flesh, ye shall die: but if ye through the Spirit do mortify the deeds of the body, ye shall live. – Rom. 8:13

So put to death the sinful, earthly things lurking within you. Have nothing to do with sexual immorality, impurity, lust, and evil desires. Don't be greedy, for a greedy person is an idolater, worshiping the things of this world. – Col. 3:5 (NLT)

A painful thing about lack of self-control is when people are forced to marry others because of pregnancy. Sometimes there is no love but due the fact that pregnancy has occurred, you settle in to a loveless marriage for life. Please do all you cannot to let your sexual urges be in the driving seat of your destiny. Marriage is bigger than sex. The time spent by couples having sex is a microcosm of the marriage. Couples can go for long periods of time without having sex, and even where it is happening often it may only take a few minutes of the twenty-four hours in the day. If sex is what drove you into that marriage, what are you going to do with the rest of the time?

THE AGE PRESSURE

To every thing there is a season, and a time to every purpose under the heaven: – Eccles. 3:1

Who told you, you were running late? According to whose time? Life is not a race even though it may seem that way. We are all walking our paths individually set by God. We may all be classmates in one classroom but you will hardly find any two of us who were born on the same date at the same time. Even twins are born at separate times that should tell you that the race is individual. It is therefore unwise to compare yourself with your contemporaries and judge yourself unfavourably just because others have something you do not have. Do not be too hard on yourself. The race is not for the swift.

For we dare not make ourselves of the number, or compare ourselves with some that commend themselves: but they measuring themselves by themselves, and comparing themselves among themselves, are not wise. – 2 Cor. 10:12

What happens when you put yourself under the pressure of time is that you become willing to sell yourself to the nearest available bidder. You sell yourself cheap only to wake up after getting married and realise that you have made a mistake. Consumable products that are manufactured in factories usually have a sell by date by which if they are not sold, the seller is forced to reduce the price to get rid of them quickly to avoid a total loss as well as the disposal cost. Thankfully, you are not a product made by man. You are beautifully, fearfully and wonderfully made by God for a purpose, and as long as God lives, you will live to fulfil your purpose in His time.

I returned, and saw under the sun, that the race is not to the swift, nor the battle to the strong, neither yet bread to the wise, nor yet riches to men of understanding, nor yet favour to men of skill; but time and chance happeneth to them all. – Eccles. 9:11

Do not get ahead of yourself in the bid to help God and end up with long-term regrets. Remember Sarah and Abraham who could not wait for God's appointed time for Isaac, and from their impatience we see all the troubles they brought upon themselves and the rest of the world. Some people marry very early, others marry midterm and yet others marry late. What matters most is that all who want to get married will do so at the right time and live fulfilled lives. So take your time, if you feel under the age pressure, be assured that God's timing is perfect soflow with Him. You are not late.

He hath made every thing beautiful in his time: also he hath set the world in their heart, so that no man can find out the work that God maketh from the beginning to the end. – Eccles. 3:11

THE FINANCIAL PRESSURE

Two are better than one; because they have a good reward for their labour. – Eccles. 4:9

It is true that marriage has financial benefits, in fact, quite a lot of benefits. At least you stop paying two rents, two utility bills etc... Also because of the doubled force of labour, you get more done and receive more returns on your usual daily activities. That said, this is only true when both parties pull their weight. The marriage that works is made up of two individuals who both bring quality to the table and are willing to sweat it out for success; not when one comes in just to milk the other. It is a very bad decision to get married with the primary intention of getting out of your financial problems. Marriage does not cure poverty. Poverty is a spirit. Poverty is a mind-set. If you have it, no amount of access to a rich spouse's wealth will make you prosper. It will all be superficial and wane once you're found out and sent packing. If you hang around for a little longer, you will infect the whole marriage with this spirit of poverty and ruin everything. If you are suffering from poverty, deal with it. Seek the right ways of breaking the curse other than handouts. Handouts have never made anyone rich. It is what you produce yourself that does.

He that loveth silver shall not be satisfied with silver; nor he that loveth abundance with increase: this is also vanity. – Eccles. 5:10

Marry to add value. Never have the mentality of the gold digger. It devalues you and turns you into an object. It is a subtle form of selling yourself into slavery. You will never have the voice of a legitimate spouse. The money will be your god and it will be visible to any wise person. Most people who venture into this kind of marriage end up in a loveless relationship where they are added to the furnishings of the house. They are often bored and frustrated, and eventually realise that money is not all that makes life tick. You are far better off in a marriage where you both love each other dearly even if there is not much money than to sell yourself off into marriage for money. You are better than that.

He becometh poor that dealeth with a slack hand: but the hand of the diligent maketh rich. – Prov. 10:4

THE SOCIAL PRESSURE

Human beings are created to relate to other human beings. God saw that it was not good for the man to be alone. He therefore made a woman, who was also not made to live alone but to relate to the man and to help him. The help that we get from each other are mainly relational as the closer we are with people, the more help we get from them.

Unfortunately, relating with people also has its down sides. People often have an opinion about everything and they often believe that what they think is the only right way. This means that they tend to judge others based on their own limited beliefs. They therefore tend to question you as to why you have not met the standard they expect of you, and may even go on to counsel you as to what to do in order to meet their expectation of you, most often without you soliciting their counsel. I have a friend who always has a word of advice for me on everything even though he doesn't live in the United Kingdom. Anytime he visits, he talks as if he is the one who lives here and we are the visitors. He will tell us what to do about everything for which we have not complained or asked for his input. It is so funny, my wife and I just laugh it off.

And it came to pass, when she pressed him daily with her words, and urged him, so that his soul was vexed unto death; –Judg. 16:16

Samson lost his freedom, strength and eyes due to pressure from Delilah. If you do not develop a strong self confidence, people will push you into doing what you do not want to do, or that which may not be God's will for your life and you will end up with long-term regrets. Avoid being intimidated by those "are you married yet", "when are you getting married", "why haven't you shown us anyone yet" etc… questions. If you don't, they will lead to the "I know someone who will suit you", "I know a prophet or voodoo man who can help you" suggestions. Be confident in yourself. Remember that it may not be good to be alone but that does not mean you are incomplete on your own. When God made man, He looked and said it was good before He thought of the help meet. The fact that you have no help meet as yet does not mean that you are bad.

For do I now persuade men, or God? Or do I seek to please men? For if I still pleased men, I would not be a bondservant of Christ. – Gal. 1:10

Do not be intimidated by friends who show off their spouses on social media, at Church, at parties and at the work place. God is working things out for your good, so do not take what you see on social media as reality. Many fake lifestyles are displayed on these social platforms. Fret not thyself. Avoid people who give you unnecessary pressure, enjoy your own company and thus your life.

For I know the thoughts that I think toward you, saith the LORD, thoughts of peace, and not of evil, to give you an expected end. – Jer. 29:11

THE FAMILY PRESSURE

There is nothing as painful as seeing your younger sister or brother getting married whilst you are being sent on errands as the unmarried and hence available one. The pressure becomes real when your mother starts asking about your own potential spouse. Sometimes she means no harm, as you are also her child and she wants the best for you,however she may not realise the pressure she is putting you through. Oh yes, even when she tells you that she is praying for you, or when she misinterprets everything you do as being jealous of your younger sibling and she tries to cool you down and counsel you. On a few occasions she may tell you off under the same theme. It is not easy. Or when you have finished school for years and are still living in yourparent'shome and they keep casting all sorts of insinuations as to when are you going to go into your own matrimonial home. How about when your mother starts asking for her grandchildren? The pressure is real!

This pressure however is not the reason why you should rush into marriage with anyone who shows up. Do you remember when Laban forced Jacob to marry Leah just because she was the first born? Do you realise she was never loved? She sometimes had to make deals in order to get Jacob to have sex with her. At some point, she was using childbirth as a means of ensuring that her husband would love her. She ended up naming her children after her situation. You do not want a loveless marriage just because you are the older one or not yet married.

You have a responsibility to do due diligence to ensure that when you leave home, you don't return the next month. I've seen many make this mistake; they try to get married just to prove a point to their parents only to return to their parents' house shortly thereafter. My friend, when it happens this way, the latter shame is greater than that of the former. Please take your time.

CHAPTER 2

AM I READY FOR MARRIAGE?

Let us be glad and rejoice, and give honour to him: for the marriage of the Lamb is come, and his wife hath made herself ready. – Rev. 19:7

One very important question to ask yourself after you have satisfied your conscience that you are not under any of the above pressures is whether you are ready for this journey. Being of age is not enough. Being beautiful is not enough and having left home or having a job is not enough.

Marriage is very demanding. Do you have a kind heart? Are you forgiving? Are you accommodating? Do you have the heart to take all the "nonsense" that it brings? Can you share the same bed with another person comfortably even when they snore and present other nuisances throughout the night? Can you easily adapt to the needs and demands of the other person? Can you share toilets and private things with another person? Are you kind enough to entertain and support the other party for life? You do not want to become a permanent pain for anyone. Are you ready? You will have to take your spouse's family as your own. Are you ready?

For which of you, intending to build a tower, sitteth not down first, and counteth the cost, whether he have sufficient to finish it? – Luke 14:28

There could be times of strong misunderstandings and tension in the home. Are you ready? You may be required to stand strong and intercede extensively and intensively for your spouse. Are you ready? There could be times when there is nothing at home to eat. Are you ready? There could be times when bills are due and there is nothing in the bank to clear them and the pressure is on. Are you ready?

Marriage is not for the faint hearted. It is not a stroll in the park neither is it a circus show. It is a tough job for tough people. It may require sweat sometimes, tears sometimes and even blood at other times. Make sure to be ready before you say I do, but be clear on this once you make your heart ready, God will make all grace available unto you. It is people like you who get married. You can do it and do it well with His help.

I can do all things through Christ which strengtheneth me. – Phil. 4:13

WHAT DO I BRING TO THE TABLE

Having confirmed that you are ready to take a serious look at marriage, you should assess yourself as to why you think you deserve to be married. Ask yourself, what do I bring to the table? Why should Brother A or Sister B marry me instead of Sister C or Brother D? What are my qualities? What are my weaknesses that I must watch out for in order not to be sent back? Beauty is not the main thing that sustains a marriage. Character is. There is s saying that even if your beauty sends you into a marriage and your character is not good, that bad character will send you back.

STRENGTHS

We are not all the same. Everyone has areas where they do well and areas where they don't excel. No one is poor at everything, therefore if you do not highlight what you are good at and project them, no one will. You are your own first ambassador. You have to show what you can do first before people will advertise you. Ask yourself some serious questions. What are the things about me that will make my marriage work? What are my strengths that I must highlight and project in every relationship or marriage that I get into in order to make me indispensable to the one who marries me? Make a list of such things and find out how you can even polish and perfect them. Maybe you have good qualities pertaining to selling, neatness, prayer and cooking. Do not underestimate these qualities. Do not think they are nothing. Work on them. Become an expert in them. Let them become the defining characteristics about you. When people mention your name, let these things come straight to their minds. You will be amazed to know that someone's most desirable trait in his or her potential spouse will be that characteristic and this will make you easily identifiable.

There is a lad here, which hath five barley loaves, and two small fishes: but what are they among so many? – John 6:9

How did the disciples know that this boy had fish at the time of their need? He had obviously not hidden it. He might have told someone about it or opened it every now and then to smell the aroma. So when the time of need came, everyone remembered him straight away. Learn to project your strengths.

And when the words were heard which David spake, they rehearsed them before Saul: and he sent for him. And David said to Saul, Let no man's heart fail because of him; thy servant will go and fight with this Philistine. And Saul said to David, Thou art not able to go against this Philistine to fight with him: for thou art but a youth, and he a man of war from his youth. And David said unto Saul, Thy servant kept his father's sheep, and there came a lion, and a bear, and took a lamb out of the flock: And I went out after him, and smote him, and delivered it out of his mouth: and when he arose against me, I caught him by his beard, and smote him, and slew him. Thy servant slew both the lion and the bear: and this uncircumcised Philistine shall be as one of them, seeing he hath defied the armies of the living God. David said moreover, The LORD that delivered me out of the paw of the lion, and out of the paw of the bear, he will deliver me out of the hand of this Philistine. And Saul said unto David, Go, and the LORD be with thee. – 1 Sam. 17:31-37

David once sought to take the opportunity to use his strengths to help Israel but people did not believe in him. His brothers did not trust him neither was the King sure of him. He did not get offended and say well if you do not believe me, carry on. He took his time to share his resume. He explained to them why he believed he was the right man for the job and enumerated the various times and places where he had excelled in that field and how he succeeded. This gave him some credibility and he was awarded the contract which eventually helped him to become King. Do not sit on your strengths, work on them and highlight them. Someone is seeking a spouse with those characteristics and will choose you for their mate.

WEAKNESSES

Just as we all have strengths, we also have areas where we are not so strong. Do not wait for people to always complain about them whilst you do nothing about it. If you don't change, you may be chosen at first but dropped along the line. Do regular self-analysis. What do people complain about me? What are the things that have annoyed people about me and what can I do about them? What are the weaknesses that I must work on? Be honest with yourself; don't just look for quick explanations, and do not be too self-defensive. Those who mention these things to you actually love you. Even if they use them as insults or rebukes, do not take the offense to heartbut look for the truth in what they are saying, thank them for their observations, then honestly see how you can improve your character. Do not make enemies of people who point things out to you. Love them instead! For in the day when it all comes pouring down, you will wish that you had listened. Love your critics; they are helping you to become a better version of yourself.

Open rebuke is better than secret love. – Prov. 27:5

Once your weaknesses have come to light by your own honest self-realisation or at the promptings of those who are closest to you, aim not to remain the same. Work on these weaknesses. Seek counsel. Read books. Go to God in prayer. Make every effort to become a better person. Make sure that your weaknesses never become what you are known for. Improve upon themuntil they are hardly visible. Do not ignore them, as they can be deadly. Take positive action; admit and correct them!

Therefore whosoever heareth these sayings of mine, and doeth them, I will liken him unto a wise man, which built his house upon a rock: And the rain descended, and the floods came, and the winds blew, and beat upon that house; and it fell not: for it was founded upon a rock. And every one that heareth these sayings of mine, and doeth them not, shall be likened unto a foolish man, which built his house upon the sand: And the rain descended, and the floods came, and the winds blew, and beat upon that house; and it fell: and great was the fall of it. – Matt. 7:24-27

OPPORTUNITIES

It is said that opportunities come but once. By this, I do not mean that when you see a man or a woman, you must jump at them and pressure them into marrying you. The meaning behind this'opportunity' phraseis that when opportunities for work and sacrifice come, take advantage of them. David had only been sent to deliver food to his brothers on the war front but when he saw an opportunity, he took it. Your willingness to serve and help will most likely bring you to the limelight for someone to see you and desire you. Do not be self-seeking, be self-giving. Yes, it was risky. Yes, he could have lost his life but nothing precious comes easy.

When you see that people are needed at Church for one thing or the other, volunteer. When they need people to do more at work, volunteer. When helpers are needed in the community, stand up and be counted. Especially when you believe you can help, take advantage of the opportunities. Many people have testified that they saw their spouses doing something selfless and were attracted to them. Do not sit down focusing only on yourself and expect that good people will come your way. Service attracts!

And David spake to the men that stood by him, saying, What shall be done to the man that killeth this Philistine, and taketh away the reproach from Israel? for who is this uncircumcised Philistine, that he should defy the armies of the living God? And the people answered him after this manner, saying, So shall it be done to the man that killeth him. – 1 Sam. 17:26-27

Please learn from a smart woman in the Biblecalled Rebekah. She knew an opportunity when she saw one and she took it and sealed her legacy in history as the mother of nations. It was just an ordinary day where she had been sent to fetch water. She met a man at the well who needed water. She could easily have said she was in a hurry. She could have offered the water with an attitude; after all she was beautiful. She however saw it as an opportunity to be of service to another. My friend, you never know which day your sacrifice and service will bring you what you need or want. So serve at all times. Take advantage of opportunities and serve. They may not always yield the desired fruit, and people may take advantage of you, but still press on and serve. Also, do not do eye service. Never serve with an expectation, you will be disappointed. Just serve. When the clouds are full of water, they empty themselves upon the earth. When your time comes, your service will showcase its reward without effort.

And it came to pass, before he had done speaking, that, behold, Rebekah came out, who was born to Bethuel, son of Milcah, the wife of Nahor, Abraham's brother, with her pitcher upon her shoulder. And the damsel was very fair to look upon, a virgin, neither had any man known her: and she went down to the well, and filled her pitcher, and came up. And the servant ran to meet her, and said, Let me, I pray thee, drink a little water of thy pitcher. And she said, Drink, my lord: and she hasted, and let down her pitcher upon her hand, and gave him drink. And when she had done giving him drink, she said, I will draw water for thy camels also, until they have done drinking. And she hasted, and emptied her pitcher into the trough, and ran again unto the well to draw water, and drew for all his camels. And the man wondering at her held his peace, to wit whether the LORD had made his journey prosperous or not.

And it came to pass, as the camels had done drinking, that the man took a golden earring of half a shekel weight, and two bracelets for her hands of ten shekels weight of gold; And said, Whose daughter art thou? tell me, I pray thee: is there room in thy father's house for us to lodge in? And she said unto him, I am the daughter of Bethuel the son of Milcah, which she bare unto Nahor. She said moreover unto him, We have both straw and provender enough, and room to lodge in. And the man bowed down his head, and worshipped the LORD. And he said, Blessed be the LORD God of my master Abraham, who hath not left destitute my master of his mercy and his truth: I being in the way, the LORD led me to the house of my master's brethren. – Gen. 24:15-28

THREATS

And Eliab his eldest brother heard when he spake unto the men; and Eliab's anger was kindled against David, and he said, Why camest thou down hither? and with whom hast thou left those few sheep in the wilderness? I know thy pride, and the naughtiness of thine heart; for thou art come down that thou mightest see the battle. And David said, What have I now done? Is there not a cause? And he turned from him toward another, and spake after the same manner: and the people answered him again after the former manner. – 1 Sam. 17:28-30

Not everyone will like you. Not everyone will believe in you. Not everyone will be pleased by your efforts. It is normal. People see things differently. It does not necessarily mean that you are not good enough. You may only not be good enough for them. There will always be the naysayers who will shout you down, but keep pressing on. What you need to do is to know how to keep your focus and to build your faith in such a way that they do not scare you. Some will say you are not beautiful enough. Some may come into your life only to find some flimsy excuse to leave you. Do not let their reason become your identity. Pick your identity from the scriptures and let that be your guide. Never allow anyone and their estimation of you to scare you out of the race. Never allow your past failures to scare you. Never allow your weaknesses to scare you. You are worth God's best. Defy the threats. David puts it beautifully in Psalm 23.

Yea, though I walk through the valley of the shadow of death, I will fear no evil: for thou art with me; thy rod and thy staff they comfort me. – Ps. 23:4

There will also be the competition. Aim to become better than them. When your service and sacrifice brings you to the limelight and someone begins to notice you and show interest, you will then see someone come from the side-linesto try to spoil your party. What is yours is yours. Do not engage them. Do not fight them. Do not allow their presence to threaten you. Stars shine brightest in darkness. This situation presents you with an opportunity to shine. This is where you focus on your best character and strengths. Never feel threatened. Do not mention them in your conversations. Just excel and persist. Set the standards so high that they fall away without a fight. Also,at this time of trial take the opportunity to pray often and to ask the Lord to fight for you.

CHAPTER 3

PROPOSAL – AT THE "DOOR" OF A RELATIONSHIP

WHEN I HAVE TO SPEAK

Every marriage begins with some sort of friendship that we generally call courtship. All courtships begin with some sort of proposal. This therefore gives the idea that a proposal is the starting point of every marriage and family, and hence must be taken very seriously. You could lose a potentially beautiful marriage as well as your peace of mind and even your feeling of manliness if your proposal goes wrong. You can imagine how it feels if the woman of your dreams turns down your genuine proposal.

There was a young and handsome university graduate who had everything a woman could wish for; let's call this young man William. Every sister in the Church and at William's work place was praying for his proposal. William was the dream husband of every woman. When everybody thought all was well with him, William thought otherwise. He spent lots of sleepless nights thinking of how he could put himself together to propose to this beautiful girl in his Church whom we will call Betty. William had once proposed to Linda, his course mate during his final year at the university, and this was a total disaster that led to feelings of low self-worth in William, which negatively impacted his ability to graduate with First Class Honours. This was an error in judgment that William did not want to repeat with Betty.

Even though a proposal is the starting point of every marriage, it is a very controversial issue which if not handled well could prevent the realisation of a potentialand genuine love-filled marriage.

According to the Collins Concise Dictionary, aProposal, is an act of proposing, a suggestion put forward for consideration, or an offer of marriage. Going by the third definition, the ultimate aim for proposing should be marriage. One must therefore be careful about whom, when, where and why they make a proposal, before embarking on this eternal journey. A proposal is supposed to lead to marriage and not frustrations and broken hearts.

BEYOND LOOKING TO SEEING!

The simple believeth every word: but the prudent man looketh well into his going. – Prov. 14:15

So many people today look without seeing. There is a difference between looking and seeing. God expects every child of His not only to look but also to see. When you look, you are hooked but when you see, you become! God wants to take you beyond the level of looking to the level of seeing.

The earlier quotation does not end by asking us to "look" but to "look well". The "look well" aspect is the realm of "seeing". There are many factors that should be considered before proposing or accepting a proposal. Some of these are spiritual compatibility, educational background, cultural background, financial position, social status, political orientation, personal hygiene and future aspirations.

CHAPTER 4

SPIRITUAL COMPATIBILITY

Before you consider anyone for the lifelong commitment of marriage, you have to ensure that you are at least compatible on the all important subject of Spirituality. The Biblestates that everything we see comes out of that which we cannot see, the spiritual realm. When there is no cooperation on the spiritual side, you are bound to struggle on the natural physical side.

Is the person you are considering for marriage a born again Christian? Are they baptised of the Spirit and of water? What are their beliefs on the so-called controversial issues such as tongues speaking, divine healing, the Holy Spirit, and baptism, the concept of the Trinity, the wearing of ornaments and make-up, the braiding of the hair and the use of hair extensions, as well as head scarves? How about the importance of tithing and giving? Be clear about their stance on such issues before you either lose your way in your walk with God or invite an unending war into your future home.

As Christians, the first thing that we have to look out for from our prospective partners is their faith in terms of which religion they belong to and how deeply involved they are in practicing their faith. We are not saying this just because we are Christians, but we have to understand that other religions equally do not permit marriage with *non-believers* of their faith or at least do not encourage marriage between their members.

Be ye not unequally yoked together with unbelievers: for what fellowship hath righteousness with unrighteousness? And what communion hath light with darkness? – 2 Cor. 6:14

This clearly states that we who profess to be under the light of Christ cannot propose to people we call unbelievers and neither can we consider their proposals no matter the other qualities that they may possess. Do not look beyond the spiritual barrier into other material or physical advantages.

For to be carnally minded is death, but to be spiritually minded is life and peace. –Rom. 8:6

If you ignore the spiritual differences in favour of carnal incentives, you will regret it in the future.People have for that matter considered the "convert and possess" as well as the "possess and convert" approaches. These approaches are however not helpful. A sister or brother who is desperately in love with you will do anything within their power, including confessing the

Lordship of Jesus Christ if that does the trick, to win your heart only to revert to their true nature after the marriage. Let not a sister or a brother come to Christ because they want you. Let them rather come to you because they have Christ. Never give them the condition of "if you love me then you have to come to my Church or you must be born again" The first question he will ask himself is "what does it take to become born again?" In actual fact this is the cheapest condition one can give in exchange for love. Don't cheapen your love. Don't give it to people who will follow Christ because they want you. You are better off with those who love you because they are in Christ already and can see that you bear the fruit of the Spirit.

Don't forget that even those of us who genuinely got born again sometimes wander off under severe circumstances. What are you going to do if after getting you to fall in love with him or her and settling in marriage, he or she returns to their old self? Are you going to leave them if you have gone as far as having children with them? Watch out! Someone out there is desperately after your love and will do anything to get it. This may include falsely becoming born again and even praying in false tongues. There has been an incident in London where a Muslim pretended to be a Christian, got seriously involved in Church activities and married the leader of the prayer department. Just a few years after the wedding and having been blessed with two children, the man claimed he had become a Muslim and insisted that his wife follow suit. They did not know that he had always been a Muslim. This is a very disturbing and embarrassing situation that is still being looked into. Sisters, be warned especially about Muslim men who are using this strategy to get Christian women to become Muslims.

For what shall it profit a man if he gains the whole world and loses his soul? –Mark 8:36

The "Possess and convert" approach is actually the most dangerous and incidentally the most common of the two. This school of thought usually quotes 1 Corinthians7:12-16 in which Paul says:

"But to the rest speak I, not the Lord: if any brother hath a wife that believeth not and she be pleased to dwell with him, let him not put her away. And the woman which hath an husband that believeth not, and if he be pleased to dwell with her, let her not leave him..."

Don't forget that Paul was talking to people who had been "Pagans" for all their lives and married in that state then either of them comes to know Christ. In this instance, we are talking about people who got married as unbelievers and one of them is now converted. You are already a believer and also yet to either propose or to be proposed to. Unfortunately, *this scripture does not apply to you.*Let us not manipulate scripture to suit our desires.

Many have encouraged themselves that their prospective unbelieving partners will get born again later after they are married. That is a big lie. This is not to say that it is not possible but will it happen at all? If they will not follow you to Church when theyhaven't won your heart yet, how do you expect them to do so after you have become theirs? Do not forget that he or she who is in love will put up their best until they finally get you. Watch out then if you are not satisfied with his or her behaviour at the time when they are seeking your love. It couldget worse after they've 'won' you. Be careful also with those who surface abruptly from nowhere and profess to have been with Christ for ages. Insist on people with a checkable Christian background. When did they get born again? Where do they go to Church? Who is their pastor? If they were true Christians, their pastor should know them well enough to be able to give a good reference. And be careful of this generation where people lie without blinking. As pastors, we have had people sit before us and lie about their

Church only for me to pick up the phone to call their pastor in their presence, then their tone changes. Others are also able to arrange with their own friends to pose as pastors to give them recommendations especially if it is only on the phone or social media. If you are going to marry a physical person, know their physical Church, physical pastor and physical spiritual references. It will save you from many troubles in the future.

Apart from Salvation, there are differences in doctrine in the body of Christ. Even though Christ should be the central pillar of our faith, some people wander off to believe in their special doctrines even more than Christ. For some people, if you do not put on a head covering, you are going to hell whether you are saved and living holy or not. Others insist that you must go to Churchon a Saturday by all means and that Sunday worship is Pagan even though the Bible says that what matters most is knowing God and living for Him but these special people will insist on certain outward religious rituals and emblems until it ruins the harmony in your home. Beware!

But now, after that ye have known God, or rather are known of God, how turn ye again to the weak and beggarly elements, whereunto ye desire again to be in bondage? Ye observe days, and months, and times, and years. I am afraid of you, lest I have bestowed upon you labour in vain. –Gal. 4:9-11

Let no man therefore judge you in meat, or in drink, or in respect of an holyday, or of the new moon, or of the sabbath days: –Col. 2:16

One man esteemeth one day above another: another esteemeth every day alike. Let every man be fully persuaded in his own mind. He that regardeth the day, regardeth it unto the Lord; and he that regardeth not the day, to the Lord he doth not regard it. He that eateth, eateth to the Lord, for he giveth God thanks; and he that eateth not, to the Lord he eateth not, and giveth God thanks.For none of us liveth to himself, and no man dieth to himself.For whether we live, we live unto the Lord; and whether we die, we die unto the Lord: whether we live therefore, or die, we are the Lord's.For to this end Christ both died, and rose, and revived, that he might be Lord both of the dead and living. – Rom. 14:5-9

Those who insist on head coverings for example only read up to verse 14 and fail to see in verse 15 that the covering being talked about is long and presentable hair and not necessarily a cloth over the hair.

But if a woman have long hair, it is a glory to her: for her hair is given her for a covering. – 1 Cor. 11:15

But long hair is a beautiful way for a woman to cover her head. – 1 Cor. 11:15 (CEV)

They also fail to recognise, that by the given analogy, the scripture may even apply to only married women and that the covering is only to honour their husbands and that it has nothing to do with God (1 Cor. 11:3-5). God is not afraid of hair. He created it. If they use the argument of having power over angels, they forget that in Christ, we already have power over angels as we will even judge them. The Bible also says that they are ministering spirits sent to minister unto us (Heb. 1:14). We do not need head coverings to have power over angels. If you marry or get into a relationship with someone who lacks a certain depth in the knowledge of the scriptures or is indoctrinated with some of these things, you will go through a lot of pain. It is not a sin to have on a head covering, neither is it a sin not to have it. Each person has the right to decide what works best for them at any given time. Those who wear it must not judge those who don't and those who don't must not look down on those who do.

Depending on your own school of thought, indoctrination and scriptural depth, you need someone who will match your set of beliefs or at least be open enough to accommodate yours without causing unnecessary rancour in the relationship or consequently, marriage. As Christians or even as human beings the most important thing we need is salvation in Christ. Most of what causes doctrinal differences and divisions are just secondary. If a person has faith in Christ and lives a holy and righteous life in obedience to scripture, they will go to Heaven.

CHAPTER 5

SPIRITUAL STABILITY

It is very important to check the spiritual weight ofthe person you intend to marry to ensure that they are on a similar spiritual wavelength as yourself. You want to ensure that your intended partner for marriageis a helper and not a helpless dependent. If you don't, you will soon realise your mistake. You will end up with an extra burden instead of extra support. Courtships and even more so marriages do face storms. Health storms, financial storms, social storms, spiritual storms, career storms as well as emotional and other storms will come. Jesus never promised us a life without storms.

I have told you these things, so that in me you may have peace. In this world you will have trouble. But take heart! I have overcome the world.–John 16:33

Troubles are part of life just as storms are part of the weather. When people build houses, they take into consideration the climate of the place where they intend to build and factor the potential stresses into the design and types of materials to use if they want it to last. It is no different when you have to choose a marriage partner. Look at the troubles in this world and envisage the potential stresses that they can bring upon your marriage and choose a partner who is strong enough both spiritually and emotionally to weather such storms should they come. If you don't, it will only be a matter of time before the whole marriage comes crashing down. It will not be the devil's fault, it will be due to your inability to carry out due diligence.

Confidence in an unfaithful (unstable) man in time of trouble is like a broken tooth, and a foot out of joint. – Prov. 25:19

As marriage counsellors, we often meet many frustrated people who are married to spouses who are not pulling their weight in the "basic weather" of their life and are hardly prepared or able to withstand the least trouble. Such marriages eventually fail when the storms of life hit. They will run away when you become sick for longer than necessary. They will run away when you are jobless for a long period. They will run away when your body shape changes. They will run away when the grass looks greener on the other side. Insist on a spiritually stable person for a spouse. God is not short of them. Do not settle for less.

STABILITY IN THE WORD

In the beginning was the Word, and the Word was with God, and the Word was God. The same was in the beginning with God. All things were made by him; and without him was not any thing made that was made. In him was life; and the life was the light of men. And the light shineth in darkness; and the darkness comprehended it not. – John 1:1-5

Everything rises and falls on the availability and application of the word of God. Everything you see around is as a result of God's word. The joys, the peace and prosperity as well as the pains, suffering and destruction all come as a result of the presence or absence of the word of God. When the word is in abundant supply and well obeyed in a person's life, it results in great prosperity and peace. On the other hand, when there is a lack of the word or its obedience, the result is poverty, pain and suffering.

Length of days is in her right hand; and in her left hand riches and honour. Her ways are ways of pleasantness, and all her paths are peace. – Prov. 3:16-17

My people are destroyed for lack of knowledge: because thou hast rejected knowledge, I will also reject thee, that thou shalt be no priest to me: seeing thou hast forgotten the law of thy God, I will also forget thy children. – Hos. 4:6

The person you intend to marry therefore must be a person who has the understanding of the importance of the word of God, and has decided to acquire and live by it, and be willing to pay every necessary cost, knowing that it will be dearer to experience the consequences of living otherwise.

Do not settle for less. Do not be quick to settle with a person who takes the word of God for granted. A person who explains everything away or laughs at his inability or unwillingness to obey God's word is a disaster waiting to happen.

IT IS YOUR WISDOM

Keep therefore and do them; for this is your wisdom and your understanding in the sight of the nations, which shall hear all these statutes, and say, Surely this great nation is a wise and understanding people. – Deut. 4:6

Human reasoning changes with time but the word of God abides forever. It is the wisdom bank; man's point of reference to live above the natural limitations of this life. A person who has little regard for God's word may seem smart in his or her own eyes but in reality, has very little wisdom. Avoid them!

Therefore whosoever heareth these sayings of mine, and doeth them, I will liken him unto a wise man, which built his house upon a rock: And the rain descended, and the floods came, and the winds blew, and beat upon that house; and it fell not: for it was founded upon a rock. And every one that heareth these sayings of mine, and doeth them not, shall be likened unto a foolish man, which built his house upon the sand: And the rain descended, and the floods came, and the winds blew, and beat upon that house; and it fell: and great was the fall of it. –Matt. 7:24-27

When a person lives by the word of God and submits to its dictates, it gives them a very strong foundation and secures their standing in the days of the storms. They can keep smiling when everyone expects them to give up. That is where David says, "*Yea though I walk through the shadows of death, I fear no evil*". Why? Because they have read, understood, experienced and are confident that Godis with them and will never let them down. A word-oriented person cannot go down with the storms no matter how hard they blow. If you want a relationship that will lead to a good and lasting marriage, go for a person who is very stable in the scriptures.

STABILITY IN PRAYER

I sought the LORD, and he answered me; he delivered me from all my fears. Those who look to him are radiant; their faces are never covered with shame. This poor man called, and the LORD heard him; he saved him out of all his troubles. – Ps. 34:4-6(NIV)

I want you to understand once again, this life is war. Only those willing to fight, end up amounting to anything. Interestingly also, even though a lot of the warfare is in the realms of wisdom, knowledge, discipline etc…, there is a higher dimension which is spiritual and can only be fought in the spiritual realms.

For we wrestle not against flesh and blood, but against principalities, against powers, against the rulers of the darkness of this world, against spiritual wickedness in high places. – Eph. 6:12

A husband or wife who understands the principles of prayer and fasting and is not lazy in putting them to practice will always be a blessing to have in your life. The storms will come. But when they do, you will have a spouse who knows where to run to even when you are not in the right frame of mind to act right. They know how to stand in the gap for you until the storm passes by. You must be a person of prayer yourself but you surely also need a spouse who loves prayer if you don't want to faint in the day of trouble.

STABILITY IN COVENANT WALK – CHURCH ATTENDANCE AND COMMITMENT, TITHING, SOUL WINNING ETC...

Life is governed by principles and covenants. If you want to be a doctor, you must go through the relevant studies. If you want to drive, you must observe certain rules. A person who cannot follow rules no matter the cost will not be able to keep their covenant with you. Marriage itself is a covenant walk. It places certain demands on its subjects, which can only be honoured by people who have exercised themselves in that way of living.

He that is faithful in that which is least is faithful also in much: and he that is unjust in the least is unjust also in much. – Luke 16:10

It is often said that "love is blind but marriage is an eye opener", and rightly so. When a person falls in love at first, they are too excited to notice anything untoward about their lover. This makes them seem to love unconditionally and overlook all faults. Unfortunately, the novelty wears off quite quickly in the marriage and reality begins to kick in. At this point, your spouse will begin to see all your natural blemishes as well as character flaws. They begin to see other people who seem more presentable and have better qualities than you. It is at this point that their understanding of covenant and the discipline of having walked in it will become important. If they have a covenant mind-set, they will continue to love you and treat you with all the respect that you deserve even though the excitement has waned.

One indicatoris the covenant of Church attendance. For true Christians, attending Church is almost mandatory. We are told not to forsake the assembling together of ourselves (Heb. 10:25). This is because it takes some level of discipline to be regular at Church. After the whole week's work, you want a day where you do not go out or at least even if you go, it will be at your own pace for fun. This is not always the case with Church. You have times of prayer, then you have to sit through an extensive period of preaching where you must stay focused. Afterwards you are expected to give towards the upkeep of God's work. If you do not love God and are not very disciplined, you will always find an excuse to miss Church. The discipline that it gives you however, now prepares you to be able to stick with a spouse and do as expected even when you feel tired or not interested. A person who has not built this kind of discipline into their lives can easily walk away from you when you have no excitement to offer. Marry a person who has a strong Church commitment. He is more likely to be committed to you too.

Being committed to Church also means that the person regards spiritual authority. Should anything happen in the relationship or marriage, they are more likely to listen to godly counsel than the one who has no regard for spiritual authority. Who is the spiritual father or mother of that person whom you intend to marry? How well do they know them? What report can they give of their faithfulness to the Church?

Obey them that have the rule over you, and submit yourselves: for they watch for your souls, as they that must give account, that they may do it with joy, and not with grief: for that is unprofitable for you. – Heb. 13:17

Tithing is another spiritual indicator of the stability of the person you intend to marry. It is not a matter of law for New Testament Christians but that of love and appreciation. The first person to tithe was Abraham and he did it even before the law of tithing came into effect in the Bible. Some may argue that it only recorded that he gave tithes once. That is because he only met the man of God once. You as a part of God's family who must meet your man of God weekly must also tithe regularly and consistently. You don't give it to the poor or any pastor you see fit. You give it to the one who serves you the word (bread) and prayer (wine) as your spiritual father. You send it to your Church. One proof that Abraham believed in tithing was that he also taught his children to do the same. Jacob vowed to tithe on everything that God blessed him with. It is an act of love, an act of appreciation, an act of discipline and an act of commitment.

And Melchizedek king of Salem brought forth bread and wine: and he was the priest of the most high God. And he blessed him, and said, Blessed be Abram of the most high God, possessor of heaven and earth: And blessed be the most high God, which hath delivered thine enemies into thy hand. And he gave him tithes of all. – Gen. 14:18-20

And this stone, which I have set for a pillar, shall be God's house: and of all that thou shalt give me I will surely give the tenth unto thee. – Gen. 28:22

When I met my wife, she was only 14 years old but she had a tithe card, which she happily and regularly filled as she gave the tithes of her increase. I was amazed. She has continued to tithe from then up until now without fail. This attitude is clearly manifested in all other areas of her life. Since I married her, she has not once threatened to leave me neither has she withheld anything from me. She's as kind as it gets with her time, energy and money.

Wherefore by their fruits ye shall know them. – Matt. 7:20

When you meet people who argue about whether tithes should be paid or not, please understand that it is not because they are knowledgeable about the word of God neither is it because they want to clean up the Kingdom of God. It is simply the overflow of the wickedness of their hearts. Most people who are against tithing are also stingy in other areas of their lives. I know a man who is vehemently against tithing. No amount of teaching has helped him to give his tithes. Would you believe that that is exactly how he treats his family too? He never gives to his wife and children, even the things expected of a father let alone those that comes out of a generous heart.

If they can withhold the tenth of their increase from the God who gives them everything, they will not blink to walk away from you in times of distress, neither will they feel any guilt withholding from you the best of their blessings. Watch out. Do not marry a stingy person. The only people whose argument against the tithe who you should believe are those who refuse to tithe but consistently give more than the worth of their tithes to God's work as a matter of principle. That is the true New Testament giving. If they are not giving more than the tenth to God's work, forget about their theological explanations, they are simply stingy and selfish. Avoid them!

Neither was there any among them that lacked: for as many as were possessors of lands or houses sold them, and brought the prices of the things that were sold, And laid them down at the apostles' feet: and distribution was made unto every man according as he had need. – Acts 4:34-35

In the same way, beware of the person who claims to believe in tithing but only does so as and when it suits them. If they can do that to God, they wouldn't struggle doing it to you.

CHAPTER SIX

EMOTIONAL STABILITY

The walk of love is a very emotional one. It is amazing to note that many things could be done to you by other people and would mean nothing to you until the one you love does it. Then it would mean the world to you. People may insult you and you could just brush it off but when your lover does a fraction of the same, you could be hurt for days.

For this reason anyone hoping to enter into a relationship that would last a lifetime should be emotionally matured enough not to be too hurt by trivial issues, as well as not to easily hurt their partner. I know of a man who likes to cry with the least offence. His wife is always frustrated; this is why marriage is not for children but the matured. It says a man shall leave his mother and father. He has to be emotionally independent before he can cleave to another. The same applies to the woman. As a marriage counsellor, I have tried to help some emotional babies in their marriages but it takes too much effort, which often ends up in failure. Do not marry an emotional baby.

For this cause shall a man leave his father and mother, and cleave to his wife; – Mark 10:7

HOW EASILY DO THEY BECOME OFENDED

And forgive us our sins, as we forgive those who sin against us. And don't let us yield to temptation. – Luke 11:4

One way to spot an emotionally unstable person is how easily they get offended over trivial issues. Some may refuse to speak to you for days for something as little as forgetting to call them at a given time. In as much as I do not condone carelessness in marriage, an emotionally matured person also understands that mistakes do happen whilst we are in this body. They make room for errors and omissions.

Once a person becomes emotionally attached to you in a relationship or marriage, their propensity to get offended multiplies at least ten times. So if they have anger issues in their normal relationships, it will be worse in their love relationships. Beware!

He that is soon angry dealeth foolishly: and a man of wicked devices is hated. – Prov. 14:17

Whoever is patient has great understanding, but one who is quick-tempered displays folly. – Prov. 14:29

HOW DO THEY REACT WHEN THEY ARE ANGRY?

Make no friendship with an angry man; and with a furious man thou shalt not go: – Prov. 22:24

Everyone gets angry at one time or the other but beware of people whose anger leads them to act physically. You have to be very smart in finding this out. Watch them from far and near. When they get angry, watch out for signs such as kicking objects by the wayside, clenching their fists, grinding their teeth or throwing or pushing things out of the way. You may be the next object of abuse.

He that hath no rule over his own spirit is like a city that is broken down, and without walls. – Prov. 25:28

Negative reaction when angry is not only physical. Watch out also for the change in language. Obviously, angry people talk differently but watch out for violence in the language as well as uncontrolled screaming and vituperations. When you pick these signs up, please advise yourself and stop yourself from going any further. Never deceive yourself into thinking that he or she will not do it to you because they love you or that they will change. Such traits only get worse with time.

Be not hasty in thy spirit to be angry: for anger resteth in the bosom of fools. – Eccles. 7:9

HOW LONG DOES IT TAKE THEM TO FORGIVE?

Another indicator of emotional maturity is how long it takes them to forgive. You have to find out if they have some long standing grudges against people that they are not prepared to let go. It may be your lot when you're married to them in the future. We all get offended when things do not go our way or as expected but a mature person understands that such things happen and makes emotional room for such disappointments. They may get hurt and brood over it for a while but if life must go on, forgiveness must also happen.

Make no friendship with an angry man; and with a furious man thou shalt not go: – Prov. 22:24

As mentioned earlier, our emotions operate with more sensitivity in marriage than in our regular relationships. If they cannot easily forgive regular people, it will be worse with you. Do not forget that whilst they are in offence mode, they will not talk with you or at least do it wholeheartedly. The danger with this is that things that need to be done willbe put on hold while you wait for their anger to subside; these could include situations that require an immediate response such as emergencies that could lead to the loss of life, loss of property or loss of a business opportunity.

An angry man stirreth up strife, and a furious man aboundeth in transgression. – Prov. 29:22

Be ye angry, and sin not: let not the sun go down upon your wrath: – Eph. 4:26

Do not let the sun go down on your anger in the above scripture simply means that you should not allow all the good in your relationship to die due to prolonged grudges. Do not end up sinning against the one you love due to your bitterness.

I know of a couple in the United Kingdom who were not talking because one was angry and wouldn't forgive. This continued for so long that they ended up sleeping in different rooms as a norm. The lady had an asthma attack one night but couldn't get help from her husband because they slept in separate rooms. She passed out and died in that room without the husband knowing about it until her body started to smell. The relationship had grown so cold that they did not even check on each other. The man had not seen the wife for days but couldn't be bothered to check on her because they were fighting. The only thing that drew him to her room was the smell. Beloved, this is what holding on to grudges can do. Avoid a person who cannot let go and do not be that kind of person.

He that covereth a transgression seeketh love; but he that repeateth a matter separateth very friends. – Prov. 17:9

And above all things have fervent charity among yourselves: for charity shall cover the multitude of sins. – 1 Pet. 4:8

HOW OFTEN ARE THEY HAPPY AS COMPARED TO BEING SAD?

A gloomy person is very hard to live with. Some people always see the glass as half empty instead of half full. They complain about everything, find faults with everything and are rarely grateful for anything. They always expect the worst in people and the worst to happen. They suspect everyone and see no good in anyone. Please avoid such people because it will only multiply when you're married to them and because you love them, it will be very hurtful. Such an attitude is often a sign of a greater underlying emotional or psychological imbalance. You have been warned!

A merry heart doeth good like a medicine: but a broken spirit drieth the bones. – Prov. 17:22

Some people can just go quiet for no apparent reason. They only talk when they want to and hold you in the bondage of forced silence when they do not want to talk. It is very controlling and very disrespectful. We all have times when we are not too eager to talk but relationships thrive on communication. We have to talk to each other even when we do not want to. A person who dictates when you can talk to them is a controlling person. Such people control what and when you can have access to them. This is not right. Watch out and avoid such people.

A merry heart makes a cheerful countenance, But by sorrow of the heart the spirit is broken. –Prov. 15:13

You need a person who can laugh and smile about mishaps. You need someone who will be very excited when things go right. You need someone who is able to engage you in warm conversations and who is able to talk even when they are going through the dark hours of life. Emotions are contagious. When one person goes gloomy, it affects the whole atmosphere. The moody person holds the entire family of spouse and children hostage whilst they are not happy, and until they are happy you are all going to have to stay in the gloomy jail. Spare yourself such frustrations. Marry a happy person.

The spirit of a man will sustain his infirmity; but a wounded spirit who can bear? – Prov. 18:14

HOW EASILY DO THEY BLAME OTHERS FOR THINGS THAT GO WRONG?

Reprove not a scorner, lest he hate thee: rebuke a wise man, and he will love thee. – Prov. 9:8

Have you seen the person who argues about every correction you try to give them? Those who insist that they have a reason for what they did or that it never happened or at least it is not as you think? Avoid them. An emotionally immature person hardly takes responsibility for things that go wrong. It is never their fault. Everything that goes wrong is because of someone else. They never say sorry. If you marry such a person, you will be frustrated.

A reproof entereth more into a wise man than an hundred stripes into a fool. – Prov. 17:10

We all make mistakes and a mature person should be able to admit it when they go wrong and boldly make every effort to make amends. Watch out for this trait. It will save you many nights of tears.

What this attitude of denial does to the perpetrator is that it excuses them from making any changes to their poor choices. People who do not accept responsibility do not make any effort to change. So if there is something they are doing to hurt you, as long as they do not see anything wrong from their side, they will not make any efforts to change, which means that they will continue doing the same thing no matter how hurtful it is to you.

HOW READILY DO THEY TAKE IT UPON THEMSELVES TO SOLVE PROBLEMS?

An emotionally matured person does not need to be told what to do when there are things that need doing. They are naturally responsible. They constantly look around to see what needs improving, what needs providing, what needs solving and who needs helping. That is the person you should seek to marry. Some people feel so entitled that they want everything to be done for them but never reciprocate. A friend in need is a friend indeed. That is the kind of friend you need for a spouse.

A friend loveth at all times, and a brother is born for adversity. – Prov. 17:17

Avoid irresponsible people. They can sit next to any problem or suffering and they will not raise a hand to help. They never offer to step in unless you ask them and then they will make a gloomy face the whole period that you're asking for their help. Some intentionally keep a stony face to prevent you from asking them for any help whilst others will always have an excuse as to why they cannot help. You rather need a person who will take the initiative to help with joy even when you have not asked. You will see this in how they do it for others around them. Never use their positive attitude towards you at the time when they're pursuing you as an indicator. They will revert to default settings once you're married. See it in how they treat those with whom they have no vested interest.

ARE THEY GIVERS OR TAKERS?

How kind is the person that you are considering for marriage? Take every care not to marry a gold digger or an eternal taker. People should not marry you because of what they can get from you. They should marry you because of who you are and even more so what they can bring to the table to make life better for you both. You should equally be careful not to marry someone because of his or her money, position or location. Marriage is not a charity project. We are in a generation where people want to use marriage to solve their own issues. If you live abroad, have a good job or are financially strong, you automatically become a target. Only immature people marry for such reasons. Avoid them!

A man once told my wife that God had called him into ministry but he was looking for a rich woman to marry so that she can sponsor him. That is not how ministry is done and that is the wrong motive for marriage. What happens when the money runs out? Will he divorce her and get another rich woman?

For if they do these things in a green tree, what shall be done in the dry? – Luke 23:31

When a person is emotionally matured even when they have a need, they will not be quick to demand things from you, especially since they have not married you. They will go to all extent to solve their own problem. The person who brings all their burdens and cares unto you in a relationship is still a child. When you marry them, they will become complete dependents and expect you to do everything for them. They will not take their jobs seriously because you'll be there to sponsor their irresponsibility. You are not marrying your child; their school fees, rents and various bills are not your responsibility. If you find out that they need help and are trying to sort themselves out, it will always be a blessing to help them but do not allow yourself to become a moneybag. If they have not married you and they need you for everything, what will they do to you when you're now their spouse? You can easily spot a giver by their willingness to help even when they are not in the best position. Consider such a person instead. Marriage requires a lot of kindness; marry a giver.

CHAPTER 7

SOCIAL STABILITY

WHAT IS THEIR RELATIONSHIP LIKEWITH FAMILY?

PARENTS

After marrying a person, you eventually become family; all the infatuations and excitement fade away and you become family. It is very important to know how the person you intend to marry treats their current family members. If they are kind, polite, accommodating and supportive of them, they are most likely to treat you the same. If on the other hand, they are harsh, irresponsible and easily provoked by them, that is your future staring right at you. You have been warned!

Remember what I told you: 'A servant is not greater than his master.' If they persecuted me, they will persecute you also. If they obeyed my teaching, they will obey yours also. – John 15:20

Do not be fooled by their explanations that a family member is so demanding, annoying etc… but that you are very nice. You are only nice because of their desire to marry you. After the desire has been fulfilled and you have become a family member, you will be next in line for the same poor treatment.

Honour thy father and thy mother: that thy days may be long upon the land which the LORD thy God giveth thee. – Ex. 20:12

Your prospective spouse must know how to honour their own parents and treat them very well and with all the respect expected of a child. If they do, it is more likely that they will honour your parents too. You must see them giving generously to their parents with their time, earthly goods and finances. If they do, it is most likely that they will do so for your own family and will not try to prevent you from doing so.

A son honors his father, And a servant his master. If then I am the Father, Where is Myhonor? And if I am a Master, Where is My reverence? Says the LORD of hosts To you priests who despise My name. Yet you say, 'In what way have we despised Your name?' – Mal. 1:6

Another thing to look out for is how they take counsel from their parents. Do they take their parents' counsel as old wives fables or do they listen respectfully and make reasonable efforts to obey? Of course they are no longer a childand have to be independent, but parents never finish their parenting role in our lives until they die. Even in their old age, they may observe one thing or the other and call you to give you counsel. A person who knows how to listen respectfully is also very likely to listen to your counsel when you're married to them. The signs are always on the wall but when we are in love, we ignore them only for them to come back and bite us in the future.

SIBLINGS

A person who will live happily with you in marriage will show signs of living harmoniously with their own siblings. You must observe all these before you make or say yes to any proposals. Are they always quarrelling? Are they always saying bad things about their siblings? That is the sign right there. You will be the next in line after you marry them. Do not say you were not warned.

Behold, how good and how pleasant it is for brethren to dwell together in unity! It is like the precious ointment upon the head, that ran down upon the beard, even Aaron's beard: that went down to the skirts of his garments; As the dew of Hermon, and as the dew that descended upon the mountains of Zion: for there the

LORD commanded the blessing, even life for evermore. – Ps. 133:1-3

OTHER FAMILY MEMBERS

The way they treat other extended family members will also indicate how they treat your own family. Do not forget that when you marry, your own brothers and sisters are still part of your family and may need your help every now and then. They will also visit your home as well as expect you to visit theirs. A person who does not know how to deal respectfully with their extended family members is very likely to put your siblings in the same category and find it hard to bring them in with any warmth.

HOW DO THEY BLOW THEIR OWN HORN?

Most men will proclaim every one his own goodness: but a faithful man who can find? – Prov. 20:6

This person you intend to marry, how do they praise themself? Are they the type of person who is always blowing their own trumpet as to how good, smart, generous, humble, helpful, handsome, beautiful etc… they are? I know a man who saysfrom the pulpit how his wife came from a poor home and that he is the one who promised to bring her to Europe and has actually done so. Things of that nature are completely unnecessary and quite humiliating but a person who feels too important in their own eyes will do them to shore up their self-importance. If you want your peace and dignity, avoid such people. They will always make you feel like a charity project. They will tell the world that you only exist because of them. If they do one thing for you or your family, everyone will hear about it.

He that keepeth his mouth keepeth his life: but he that openeth wide his lips shall have destruction. – Prov. 13:3

WHAT IS THEIR RELATIONSHIP WITH FRIENDS?

It is a great thing to have friends but one must choose friends carefully. A person who is friends with everybody will bring ruin to your marriage whereas a person who has no friends at all is also bound to be socially handicapped. We all need people; we need their help in times of difficulty and they will need us in their challenging times. That is how God has created us; that we live in harmony with people.

Be careful of an overly friendly person. Such people are usually not very reliable. You cannot please everybody. When you make friends with all, you end up disappointing some. And most importantly, an overly friendly person will end up sacrificing their own family in order to satisfy their friends. You will be the one to suffer that pain. I have seen husbands leave their house with a phone call from a random friend and not returnhome until the next day; some return drunk whilst others return with unplanned debts and future calls of pregnancies. Beware of the overly friendly person.

A man that hath friends must shew himself friendly: and there is a friend that sticketh closer than a brother. – Prov. 18:24

What you need is a person who takes their time to make friends and keeps such friendships for as long as it takes. Such a person is commitment oriented. They will do the same for you.

HOW LONG DO THEY KEEP FRIENDSHIPS?

When people get close to you with the aim of courting you or before you get close to someone with such an intention, find out how long they keep their friendships. You do not need a person who changes their friends the same way they change their clothes. Such a person is not consistent. You see them today so close with John only to find out that they ended the friendship over some flimsy issue and are now very close with Evan. When you marry such a person, they will treat you in the same way. When they are happy, they will hail you and be all over you. When on the other hand you offend them, which you will, they will behave as though you do not exist. That is where you will see them laughing with other ladies at Church whilst you stand by like a leper. They will spend hours on the phone with friends whilst they do not even respond to your greetings. You need a person who is stable in friendships.

My son, fear thou the LORD and the king: and meddle not with them that are given to change: – Prov. 24:21

WHAT DO THEY SAY ABOUT OTHERS IN THEIR ABSENCE?

A talebearer reveals secrets, But he who is of a faithful spirit conceals a matter. – Prov. 11:13

Beware of talkative people, backbiters and talebearers if you care about your secrets. We all have moments when we let ourselves go and chat our hearts out, but a person who is always talking is very dangerous to deal with. It is even more so when they love to talk about others and the more so when all they say about others is evil. Such people will always tell you how good you are to your face and say something else when you turn around. You can be with such people and they say very nice things to a person only for them to change their tone as soon as the person leaves. Be very careful about such people.

He that goeth about as a talebearer revealeth secrets: therefore meddle not with him that flattereth with his lips. – Prov. 20:19

If they do it to their friends, they will do it to you. You will be surprised to hear all of your issues set out the day you have a little tiff with your sister-in-law. Some will even go to great lengthsin giving out such private information to members of the Church which can affect the way they receive you, especially when you are a leader or an active member in any way. You need a man or woman who knows how to keep their mouths shut. You need a person who has some level of integrity with their lips.

WHAT IS THE GENERAL THEME OF THEIR CONVERSATIONS ABOUT PEOPLE – POSITIVE OR NEGATIVE?

Beware of people who have a critical spirit. Some people are always saying something bad about someone, sometimes even about people they have never met. They condemn political authorities, popular pastors, successful businessmen and women and almost anyone who comes to mind. Such a spirit drains and attracts demons into the atmosphere.

He that is void of wisdom despiseth his neighbour: but a man of understanding holdeth his peace – Prov. 11:12

A critical person finds faults with everybody but themselves. They are negative and retrogressive. To him or her, every successful person is in the occult, a thief or just plain lucky. They fail to give honour to whom honour is due. You cannot go far in life with such people. They will transfer it to you in the marriage. They will always be on your case. Please let them go quietly if you want peace.

WHAT DO PEOPLE WHO KNOW THEM SAY ABOUT THEM?

And the child Samuel grew on, and was in favour both with the LORD, and also with men. – 1 Sam. 2:26

If you want to marry someone and everyone has a bad report about them, beware! You will always find one person or the other who will have something negative to say but if the majority of people say bad things about a person, there might be some truth in it. Even Jesus grew in favour with men. You need a person who has some level of goodwill among people.

And Jesus increased in wisdom and stature, and in favour with God and man. – Luke 2:52

Do not become so blinded by love so as to ignore all these signs, otherwise you will find yourself in trouble later. This is why you should not entertain anyone who has no one who knows them well. Others must know the person you marry and the majority of them must have a good report of them. Play it safe. Never entertain a person who shows up from nowhere to court you even if they say God sent them to you.

Moreover he must have a good report of them which are without; lest he fall into reproach and the snare of the devil. – 1 Tim. 3:7

CHAPTER 8

THE SOCIO-CULTURAL DETERMINANTS

EDUCATIONAL BACKGROUND

Education is very important in this modern world. Computers, for example, are taking over lots of jobs, which were previously done by human beings. To be successful in this computer age therefore requires at least, some basic ability to read and write. What is your own level of education? What is your prospective partner's level of education? Are you sure that the two of you can live together without any problems? Remember also that we communicate based on our level of experiences (education) and that when the gap is too wide there is bound to be flaws or gaps in communication which is the nerve centre of every successful marriage.

Imagine the home of a highly educated and successful businessman who is married to a woman who has never had access to any formal education. How is she going to answer phone calls from his international partners? How is she going to handle various receipts, documents and other relevant business materials she finds in the house? How is she going to deputise for her husband in times of emergency? Education is therefore a very important factor to consider before any proposal.

A story is told of a highly educated and very successful businessman who received a reciprocate visit from his international partners. At the table in the morning, he prays in his local language so his visitors will not understand what he really means. And it goes:

"My sweet and lovely wife Ama, you know these people have come from afar and are not used to our local dishes hence this strange breakfast which you are also not used to. Now, my plea is that, sip the tea first, and then take a bite of the sliced bread alternatively in a very gentle manner. I beseech you by the mercies of God not to dip the bread in the tea. And as I end this strategic prayer, please say Amen and not O.K. Amen."

You can imagine how uncomfortable this man was throughout his partners visit to his home because of his uneducated wife. This is just the tip of the iceberg. There are innumerable stories of embarrassment caused by uneducated partners at various gatherings and even in the house. The same goes for people who have married the "super educated" who make them feel like trash because of their lower level of education. Do not go into a marriage where you will be made to feel unworthy! Isaiah 33:6 states:

"And wisdom and knowledge shall be the stability of thy times, and strength of salvation: the fear of the Lord is his treasure."

This scripture clearly emphasises the importance of knowledge which mainly comes from education be it formal or informal. One can hardly survive in these modern times without a working level of education. Education is good. Go for it.

This is not to say that everyone should go round looking for the "Harvard, Oxford or Cambridge" graduate. It is better for you to find someone within your "comfort zone" with whom you feel neither superior nor inferior. Don't necessarily go in for the professor but the one who can at least read and write averagely. Open your eyes wide; find the right educational fit for you.

CULTURAL DIFFERENCES

Another thing, which is not too important and yet can be extremely thorny, is the racial-cultural issue. We marry into families even though it is ultimately the object of your love that you will mostly be associated with. Differences in races can lead to loads of problems in courtship and marriage even if you both understand yourselves. Discord from extended families can severely hamper the success of your relationship. This is because various races have different ways of socialising. This accounts for the reason why to some Nigerian tribes, it is disrespectful to greet an elderly person without prostrating. This is however very strange to the English. How do you expect Sara White to prostrate before Mr. Balogun on the streets of London just because he is an in-law? Some tribes and races insist on marriage within itself whilst others are a bit more liberal. How comfortable is a German who has never tasted Akple going to feel with a beautiful Ewe lady who has spent her entire life in Kpetoe? There is definitely a problem to face when you decide to marry across tribes and races but these are not insurmountable. This is why you must know where you are going before you set off. Once you agree to ignore tribal and racial differences let them be gone. It hurts to always be made to feel inferior once the relationship has started. Take time to learn from your partner and make room for more surprises as they have been the way they are for years before you met them. Make plans also to do a lot of explaining to your family on your prospective spouse's behalf as well as on your own family's behalf.

Even though we are both black and from the same country, Ghana, I am a Fante and Selgelia is a Ga. In spite of the fact that we agree on spiritual issues and also have the same educational background, we almost always disagree when it comes to speech and its meaning. I sometimes take simple statements and comments she makes for insults because of my strict Fante upbringing. She on the other hand, thinks I am too mean. All the same, we try to understand each other no matter how uneasy it becomes. Adjusting to each other and respecting tribal and racial backgrounds irrespective of how much it will cost you is very essential for the success of your relationship and therefore, marriage. Don't allow anyone to discourage you about someone's race or tribe. After all, we are all heavenly citizens and that is the most important issue. If you really feel the love, go ahead, be ready to pay the price and take what belongs to you.

FINANCES

How easy can it be for Lizzy Fowler, the billionaire's daughter to marry Kwame Nsiah, the poor boy from the village? Who submits to whom in such a situation irrespective of what the Bible says? The Bible says that wives should submit but the same Bible also says that money answers all things. Don't forget that money is a very necessary tool in these our capitalist economies and for that matter in marriage. A Christian brother has always said "money is the wheel of the gospel". If this statement is anything to go by, then consider how important money is to your life, relationships and marriage.

A feast is made for laughter, and wine maketh merry: but money answereth all things.– Eccles. 10:19

Almost everything we do in life revolves around money and for that reason he who has more money automatically seems to be in control. There is an adage that states *"he who calls the tune pays the piper".* So if you don't have money to pay the piper, you don't call the tunes. Now, how can one call the tunes in courtship or marriage when he doesn't have money to pay for them? He who has money therefore automatically dominates the relationship irrespective of their role in the marriage. One can argue that this law does not apply to Christians forgetting that Christians also live in the capitalist economies where money dominates everything and is essential even in the Church. Who said money is not good? Saying this, we do not mean that a richer wife can never submit to her man; however, it takes a spirit filled woman to submit in this instance.

On the other hand, Billy Joe, the tycoon who feels his money can do everything is sometimes tempted to think that Mary, his wife, is one of the fleet of cars he's bought and would want to use her in that manner. Many rich menfind it difficult to respect their partners with poor financial background.

Careen and Ben had been happily married for many years until she suggested one day that they should move to a bigger house. Careen was a civil servant and Ben, a business executive. This suggestion infuriated Ben who asked Careen in anger how much money she contributed to the running of the house. Careen was very hurt and has vowed never to bring up any suggestion that has anything to do with money until she becomes rich herself.

Money can be a major cause of discord in marriage and prospective partners should look out for the financial backgrounds and possibly future financial trends of their partners and be satisfied with it before they embark on this special journey. Although money is essential, it is not all that glitters that is gold. There are many situations when money has let its owners down woefully. You are better off with the man or woman with whom you can strive to succeed together than the "already made ones".Beware of a person who wants to be in a relationship with you because of money. Instead, respect those who love you just the way you are and are prepared to go all the way with you. They are the real ones; never let them down when you are on top. Hard work pays. If a person is daring and has plans that are specific, measurable and achievable given their efforts and abilities, stick with them. God will one day crown those efforts with success. Beware of people who build castles in the air. They are vain and self deceiving. Proverbs 12:11 states:

"*He who works his land will have abundant food, but he who chases fantasies lack judgment.*"

SOCIAL STATUS

One thing worth noting also is the social status of the family of your potential spouse. Men especially have had tough times trying to win the hearts of ladies who happen to be from a higher social background.

Marcus lives in a poor suburb of Accra. His parents who are poor wage earners struggled to pay for his education up touniversity level. Whilst on campus his superb academic abilities endeared him to Julia, the daughter of one of the most prominent politicians in the country. Julia loves him and doesn't care about his background. Fear had however gripped Marcus so much that although he equally loved her and thought it was a good opportunity to climb up the social ladder, he declined the offer when she proposed. He could not imagine himself going through police checks just to visit the woman he loved. Let us not even talk about taking her out in the company of a bodyguard.He finally succumbed after so much pressure from Julia who promised not to let that difference come between them. When both families got to know of their intentions, Julia's father felt insulted while Marcus' mother thought that her son was going mad.

What would you do if you found yourself in Marcus' shoes? What if you were Julia?

This story is not an isolated case. Many potential lovers have had their dreams vanish into thin air because of the extreme differences in their social positions. We believe that a person's real social standing is what he has been able to achieve himself and not what he was born into. The high achievers in society will also have to understand that wherever they find themselves now is by the grace of God. They should therefore not lord it over the so-called low achievers in society. They must not forget that no condition is permanent and that the tides can change. Ecclesiastes 10:7 reads:

"I have seen slaves on horseback, while princes go on foot like slaves."

This not withstanding, we are Christians and the most important thing that binds us together is Christ and His love. There will not be any place assigned to the bourgeoisies when we go to heaven. In heaven there will be no room for social stratification. Why not try to live with that concept of equality now so that you will not feel bad in heaven when you are seated on the same table with someone who was a pauper on earth. Do you know that that ill feeling could cause you to be cast down? Remember Lucifer.

For who makes you different from anyone else? What do you have that you did not receive? And if you did receive it, why do you boast as though you did not? – 1 Cor. 4:7

For by one Spirit are we all baptised into one body, whether we be Jews or Gentiles, whether we be bond or free; and have all be made to drink in one spirit. – 1 Cor. 12:13

Let the sisters who are blessed with fat social backgrounds humble themselves to lowly brothers who have vision and are prepared to die for it. Also let the brothers who are sure that they are serious in life be bold and cross all social barriers no matter how tough it seems and God will do the rest. Don't be afraid of the naysayers. For dust we all are and to dust shall we all return irrespective of our current positions on earth.

CHAPTER 9

SACRIFICE TO SATISFY

WATCH OUT! IT MIGHT BE COSTLY

Before you commit yourself to any relationship, you must ask yourself, whether or not you are ready to pay the price. To satisfy your spouse, you must be ready to sacrifice. Your level of sacrifice will determine the level of your satisfaction. Never expect everything to be perfect with your spouse. You must study the person and be ready to bear all the shortfalls that come with them. There are some major issues that need to be taken into consideration; this is where you are either ready to 'pay the piper' or not!

HEALTH ISSUES

One very important thing to consider before proposing to a partner is the issue of health. This is one issue that people are reluctant to talk about. It can however make or unmake one's marriage and thereby one's life, depending on how well or otherwise it is dealt with. There are factors to consider such as diseases that run through the family, and the possibilities of transmission, blood groups of both partners, unappealing characteristics that may have health origins, physical disabilities, and past relationships of the prospective partner.

In my final year at university, I had a friend who was so much in love with a man she was courting. They made all the necessary preparations for marriage. They had taken a test to determine their blood group and sickling status. The sickling test showed that they both had the sickle cell trait – AS. People with the sickle cell trait (AS) usually do not have any of the signs of the disease, but can pass the trait on to their children.The doctor gave them the option of deciding not to marry or choosing to live with the difficulties involved in raising children who may have the sickle cell disease. My friend was very heartbroken, and breaking up with the man was a very difficult decision to make. It is critical to find out about some of these issues before a relationship becomes fully developed so as to help prevent such broken-heartedness.

BLOOD GROUPS AND COMPATIBILITY

Just as people are born with different skin colour or hair texture, we inherit a particular type of blood from our parents. Each of us is born with one of the four main blood groups: A, B, AB and O. The difference between these blood groups is the presence or absence of blood cells of certain specific markers (antigens), and the presence or absence of corresponding antibodies (proteins in blood that react with antigens).

Antibodies may react with antigens when bloods of different and incompatible groups are mixed together. The mixing of incompatible blood often results in severe illness, and sometimes, death. Blood from two different people may mix together when someone is given a blood transfusion or during pregnancy and childbirth. However, sexual intercourse in itself does not mix blood, and therefore a man and a woman having different blood groups does not mean they cannot marry each other.

Another inherited difference in blood is the presence or absence of the Rh (sometimes called Rhesus) factor. This is particularly important for childbirth, because if a woman with Rh-negative blood conceives a child with Rh-positive blood (which was inherited from the father), it can lead to problems for her subsequent pregnancies. This is why couples must be counselled on antenatal care, so that the doctors and nurses plan in advance to prevent complications during childbirth.

Everyone is born with a specific blood type and a rhesus factor, so giving someone blood from the wrong blood group can be fatal. This has implications for childbearing. If a woman has rhesus negative blood and the man has rhesus positive blood, then it is possible for problems to arise for both mother and baby. Blood screening can inform prospective couples whether this is a potential risk and an injection can be given to the mother to prevent complications. When a mother's blood type is Rh negative, but her unborn baby's is Rh positive, it can become a problem if the baby's blood enters the mother's bloodstream—for instance, during childbirth. The baby's D antigens will be identified as foreign, with the mother's body producing antibodies against them. This isn't usually a problem for the first baby, but it can be a problem for all later pregnancies where the baby is Rh positive.If antibodies produced by the mother attack the unborn baby's red blood cells, the unborn baby's damaged red blood cells may not be able to carry oxygen around their body. This could result in miscarriage or stillbirth or other complications.

GENETIC DISEASES

Sickle Cell Disease is a disorder of the blood that can be passed on to children if the parents have or are carriers of the disease. People with sickle cell anemia inherit two copies of the sickle cell gene, one from each parent (SS). People who inherit only one copy of the sickle cell gene (from one parent) will not have sickle cell anemia. They will have sickle cell trait (AS).

For instance, when two people who are AS marry, every time the woman conceives there is a 25% chance that the child will have sickle cell anaemia (SS), 25% that the child will be AA, and 50% chance that the child will have sickle cell trait (AS). However, because these are probabilities, one AS-AS couple can have their first two children being SS, while for another AS-AS couple none of their five children is SS.

There are other inherited diseases like thalassaemia and cystic fibrosis among others. Talking this over with your health specialist could be the best thing to do. Watch out.

PAST RELATIONSHIPS

Situations arise in which a partner may have been previously involved in an intimate relationship. This raises the probability of sexually transmitted diseases. There is global awareness of HIV and AIDS, especially as it is ravaging some nations. Some diseases like Chlamydia however, are very subtle, and the affected partner may not exhibit any symptoms. This is misleading, as there is a high risk of sterility. Screening is recommended as multiple tests can be done on just a few samples taken from partners.

We are not trying to say that people with such blood groups or past intimate relationships should not marry but why should you expose yourself to these problems when it could be avoided? Please do all you can to ensure that you are entering into a safe relationship. In saying this, we don't intend to nullify the word of God about faith. With God, all things are possible and therefore if a potential partner has genuine faith and can believe God for a miracle in such a situation, we will not discourage such a person. One should however be careful not to be misled by lust into such a problem where his faith is not elastic enough to stretch to the end; these people often end up blaming God when the realities begin to set in. It is understandable that there are people who are extremely compatible while others are not but it is doubtful that there is just one particular woman created for each man. Trust God to get you another person whom you will love better than this man who has a blood group that is not compatible with yours. Going ahead with the relationship could give you both heart-breaking problems. RememberProverbs 2:11:

"Discretion shall preserve thee, understanding shall keep thee."

PHYSICAL DISABILITIES OR CHALLENGES

Next on our health list comes physical disability. This is one issue that is very worrying and worthy of noting. The Bible makes it clear in 1 Samuel16:7:

"But the Lord said to Samuel, "Do not consider his appearance or his height, for I have rejected him. The Lord does not look at the things man looks at. Man looks at the outward appearance, but the Lord looks at the heart."

Truthfully speaking, the spirit filled man hardly looks at the physical configuration of the person he is dealing with. Human beings are more of spirit than body. The body is just the container of the actual substance. Will you prefer a fake chocolate drink in an excellent container to the original or genuine drink in a sachet or an unattractive container? The fact of the matter is that, it is the actual product that you need and not the container. Many have been deceived into marrying beasts in attractive bodies. Open your eyes and think twice before your excitement is exchanged for the deepest form of depression.

Disability is not inability. One of America's most famous presidents who led them through the Second World War, Franklin D. Roosevelt, was disabled. This was a man who believed against all doubts that America could redeem its poor image of being playboys who depended on Britain and Russia for their military exploits. This he proved by organising one of the most unthinkable retaliatory attacks on Japan after the latter had sunk the entire American fleet based at Pearl Harbour.

There are many successful people in life who live with various kinds of disabilities. In one European country, there is a blind man who holds a very key ministerial position and is doing excellently. Look beyond the body with its blemishes and you will be glad you did.

Charm is deceptive, and beauty is fleeting; but woman (or man) who fears the Lord is to be praised. –Prov. 31:30

Are you prepared to remain with someone whose face or shape is driving you crazy now, should an accident deform him or her? There are uncountable stories of this nature all around us. You might regret it woefully if your partner loses that particular look which attracted you to them. Mind you, those looks are in reality, fleeting. Although you will be sorry, your heart will never ache if the person you genuinely love loses any part of the body during this rough journey of life. We are not scaring you, but love transcends the'feelings' you have towards that man or woman. Will you continue to love her if she loses her teeth or one of those beautiful breasts through cancer? What if the long hair is lost through burns? Will you still be dreaming of that stout man if he is crippled through an accident or loses his sight as a reaction to some medication? What if he is totally paralysed due to a fall? If your answer is yes to any of these questions, then don't be troubled if you have to start the journey of marriage with a partner who is already suffering from any of these problems. If you can endure this during marriage, why can't you start with it if you have to?

Another health issue is diseases that are passed from parents to offspring; all human beings born of women have genes in their blood, which they inherited from their parents who in turn also inherited them from their parents. A gene, according to the Collins Concise Dictionary, is a unit composed of DNA forming part of a chromosome, by which inherited characteristics are transmitted from parent to offspring. This means that various traits in couples including diseases could be passed on to their offspring. Hypertension or high blood pressure, sickle cell anemia, diabetes, HIV-AIDS, and some kinds of mental disorders are just a few of the many diseases which are hereditary. The well-informed person makes the best decisions, it is said. Getting this relevant information about your prospective partner will be very helpful. In cases like HIV-AIDS and Sickle Cell Anemia as well as all the other diseases, we recommend that you consult a health specialist who can give the appropriate advice as to what you must do next. Once again, a careful interplay of faith and wisdom is highly recommended.

To draw the curtain on health issues, let us discuss the turn offs, which come as a result of ill health.

Jimmy, Belinda's fiancé had almost broken up with her due to her bad breath until she agreed to his persistent request for a visit to the doctor. An x ray revealed a damaged nasal bone, which was linked to a fall she had on a staircase as a baby. Jimmy's love for Belinda was rekindled as resentment gave way to compassion.

Many people find themselves in similar or even worse situations. Health problems such as sinusitis, gum bleeding, allergies, stress, fractures on the skull due to accidents, reaction to medication and diabetes could all lead to bad breath. You will make the world a better place if you learn to live with these people in compassion instead of adding to their woes with your depressing comments and gestures. It could happen to you at any time.

Apart from bad breath, there are other turn-offs like discoloured teeth, body odour, skin diseases, foot rot, stammering and excessive perspiration. Understanding their causes and finding solutions to them would be the best you could do for a loved one rather than to shun such a person. Some of these problems should not discourage you from proposing or going ahead to marry a person you genuinely love. After all, Jesus our perfect example loved us when we were full of filth as sinners. He did not despise us but gave his life so we may partake in his glory. God will bless you if you love genuinely and not selfishly. Don't forget that you receive when you give. Showing this kind of love will therefore prompt your partner to go all out for you, responding to your love as the Church is doing to Christ. This is real love. God bless you for being a doer and not just a reader.

PARTNER'S LOVE HISTORY

To help live appropriately with your partner, there is the need for both of you to lay your cards of past relationship down as honestly as possible. It will be in the interest of both of you to talk about any past relationship either of you might have entered into, how it was handled, problems encountered and what might have led to it'sbreak down. This will help you to understand your partner better. Certain people because of painful disappointments in past relationships behave quiet abnormally and sometimes want to punish you for sins you have not committed. Lamentations 5:7 states:

"Our fathers sinned and are no more and we bear their punishments."

Getting to know your prospective partner's past relationships and problems they encountered will help you to make the most reasonable decisions taking into consideration your own strengths and weaknesses as well as experiences.

Checking their love history will also help you to know the character of the person you are considering for marriage. Some people do not simply have what it takes to stay in a lasting relationship. This may be due to poor character, evil forces or even a curse which could be self-imposed or superimposed. This problem can be solved by prayer, counselling, deliverance where appropriate and personal efforts to change some unhealthy habits.

One might also try to know the sex history of the prospective partner. A person who has had quiet a good number of unprotected or careless sexual encounters definitely stands the risk of having acquired some sort of a sexually transmitted disease such as gonorrhoea, syphilis, and the worst of them all, HIV-AIDS. The fewer sexual experiences one has had, the safer they might be and vice-versa. This will also reveal any previous abortions caused, if any, the conditions under which they were committed and the possible consequences. Based on these, one can take his or her own decisions and abide by the consequences without blaming anybody. We will however advise that people who have poor history but are now in Christ and have genuinely repented should be given the necessary support and fair treatment. Remember 2 Corinthians 5:17 states:

"Therefore, if anyone is in Christ, he is a new creation; the old has gone, the new has come!"

Now if you are going to investigate someone's track record, you must also be prepared to give all the necessary information about yourself. Don't hide yours and look out for others'. If a prospective partner is seeking vital information from you, do not lie and do not put them off. Do unto others, as you will want them to do unto you. Also if you are investigating in order to make a well-informed decision, let your findings end with you. People often lay hold of vital information about people and put them on the market for public consumption. This is highly unchristian and outrageously uncouth. You must also be sure about the person to whom you are revealing yoursecrets. Do you trust them enough? Now as you investigate, be sure that your own records are also being set as straight as possible. Don't expect to get the best when you are not actually giving out the best. Always remember that it is your high level of imperfection that has paved the way for such an imperfect person into your life.

CHAPTER 10

TEMPERAMENTS

We recommend that you investigate the temperament of your prospective partner before you ask for their hand in marriage. One may now ask what the word temperament really means. In the middle ages, man was seen as a microcosm of the universe whose behaviour was determined by his physiology, which was, in turn, subject to planetary and terrestrial influences. Four different kinds of behaviour or temperament were recognised. Each was governed by the preponderance within the body of one of four particular fluids, or humours, secreted by organs. Individuals, because of astrological influences, would be naturally inclined throughout their life to one particular temperament. The four temperaments are: Phlegmatic, caused by preponderance of phlegm in the body; Sanguine by blood; Choleric, by bile (or choler); and Melancholic, by black bile. Each of the four temperaments was in turn related to the four seasons, the four elements and four animals whose nature were thought to exemplify the specific temperament: Phlegmatic to winter, water and the lamb; Sanguine to spring, air and the ape; Choleric to summer, fire and the lion; and Melancholic to autumn, earth and the pig.

The phlegmatic is described as calm, apathetic, bovine, cold, indifferent, sluggish, lymphatic, undemonstrative and unemotional. Knowing who they are will help you not to worry your head off when they demonstrate what is actually normal with them. You will be well informed not to think that he doesn't love you when he fails to respond to your moves appropriately. The phlegmatic should however read Proverbs 13:4and quicken his soul:

"The *sluggard craves and gets nothing, but the desires of the diligent are fully satisfied."*

The sanguine is also described as a cheerful, assured, buoyant, lively, confident, hopeful, optimistic and a spirited person. They are also sometimes referred to as talkative and will always find something to say about anything. Don't be moved by many of their statements. They don't really mean any harm. The sanguine must however learn to know when to talk and when to hold his peace.

Even a fool is thought wise if he keeps silent, and discerning if he holds his tongue. – Prov. 17:28

The choleric is better described as irascible, angry, bad-tempered, irritable, petulant, testy, and touchy. You must also not misinterpret their mood for a personal dislike for you. They love you but may find it hard to be soft spoken and romantic. Don't be tempted to think that they have no feelings. They do feel just like you do. They must however remember that in Ecclesiastes 7:9, the Biblestates:

"Do not be quickly provoked in your spirit, for anger resides in the laps of fools."

The melancholic, the last and the most complex of all the temperaments is better described as depressive, gloomy, low spirited, pensive, sad, dejected and despondent. Be careful what you say when the philosopher (melancholic) is around. He will definitely think it through and make a case out of it. Why not handle him with care and save him from much sorrow? The melancholic must also learn to be joyous in the salvation, which Christ has purchased for him by His blood. Proverbs 17:22 states:

"A cheerful heart is good medicine, but a crushed spirit dries up the bones."

Arise therefore O thou melancholic and be glad!

In talking about temperaments, one will have to be careful not to think that there is an absolute segregation in behaviour. After all everyone has at least once in his lifetime been angry, felt lazy and sluggish, spoken when he knew he had to keep silent and has felt sad or hurt when there was actually no basis for that ill-feeling. There is some part of each of the temperaments in every individual although the rate of concentration differs. Most often, one may have two of the four with one of them dominating the other. This accounts for the reason why some people's character cannot be easily determined. A person can be 65% choleric and 35% phlegmatic. Another can be 80% sanguine and 20% melancholic. No matter where you belong however, it is the spirit of God that you must strive to project as a child of light. How many of the fruits of the spirit have you borne since you became born again?

We started this discussion on temperaments by mentioning the fact that they originated from the Western countries in the Middle Ages and the fact that man was seen as a microcosm of the universe. These assertions are however man made and do not have any concrete hold on you as a child of God since they are not scriptural. The Bible for that matter makes us understand in 2Corinthians 5:16that:

"So from now on we regard no one from a worldly point of view. Though we once regarded Christ in this way, we do so no longer."

The children of God therefore cannot hide behind these worldly theories and glorify their weaknesses, which can be overcome by the renewal of the mind as we study the word of God in all diligence and allow His spirit to work in us. Children of God must therefore desist from the statement "*that is how I am*" and strive towards what they should be. We now know no man after his temperament but after the spirit of Christ which, works in us for the glorification of the Father as we bear the fruits of peace, love, patience, humility, long suffering, joy and service among others. However, we are put in a better position to help our loved ones if we possess a deeper understanding of their way of behaviour. You will definitely be better off if you know these factors concerning the one whom you love before you ask: will you…

BE LED

Knowledge, they say is power. The power of human knowledge can however never be compared to the power of prophecy. The Biblestates in Proverbs 16:3:

"Commit to the Lord whatever you do, and your plans will succeed."

You should not just conclude that you are well informed enough to make the best decisions. Remember, that you only know what you know, and that what you know as a man is absolutely limited. You will need to get spiritual confirmation without which you can't succeed. Go to the Lord of all secrets for the final endorsement. If the Lord who searches the hearts and all hidden things gives you the go ahead, you do not need any other information. Your diligent prayer could reveal that this person whom you are considering for marriage does not have a good spirit and you will thereby be saved. Jeremiah 33:3states:

"Call to me and I will answer you and tell you great and unsearchable things you do not know."

Go to God in your prayer closet and let him reveal to you, the actual nature of the person whom you are investigating. For it is only by this means that you will be sure of where you are going. Remember Proverbs 3:5-6:

Trust in the Lord with all your heart and lean not on your own understanding; in all your ways acknowledge him, and he will make your paths straight.

Talking about prayer reminds me of people who want to marry by visions and prophecy. There is nothing wrong with believing God for direction in your marriage. My main concern however, is that some ignorant and self-deceptive Christians cover their own selfish ambitions with the name of God. Some are genuinely in love but lack the confidence to step out and declare their intensions. Others are just lusting about and are ashamed of their intentions; hence they put the responsibility on God through prophecy. Let those who naively agree to such unscriptural proposals understand that God does not marry and as such does not fall in love with man in that respect. He however gave us heads, which contain brains, and the purpose of these brains is for both concrete and abstract reasoning. Do not abase yourselves for the manipulation of weird and inconclusive visions and prophecies. By so saying, I do not mean that prophesies and visions are not good. They are however dangerous tools, which must be used with much care before hearts are broken and the name of God is driven into disrepute. If a man has a vision or prophecy about marrying you, let God confirm it with you also before you agree to it. You are also a party to the contract and deserve to hear from God about it. Ifsomeone approaches you, saying God says, ask him, "what do you also say?" Do you personally love me or is God pushing you to marry me against your will? Watch out. Most of these people are actually not responsible, even with their feelings towards you, let alone the duties expected of them. Let them propose in their own name and not in the name of God this time. If you will live with them and not with God, let them come in their own name. Don't swallow prophecies without reason. After all, we see in part and we prophesy in part.

CHAPTER 11

A TIME FOR EVERYTHING

When the basic characteristics and factors to be aware of have been well noticed, and you are convinced about what you aregetting into, the proposal can be made without any doubts. It is not fair for a young man to "cage" a woman and assume he is in a relationship with her when he has actually not made his intentions clear. In all likelihood, the woman may be waiting for a proposal without assuming anything. Assumptions are not the best method when it comes to dealing with human beings and emotions. You should not assume that the person loves you when in actual fact they have not said yes to your proposal. Their feelings for you could be one of mere friendship. Go ahead and make your intentions known and be sure and convinced of a positive response before your heart is broken. Don't assume!! Be sure.

Jenny, a young and beautiful secretary met Alfred, a computer analyst at a business conference in Accra. They were attracted to each other. The exchange of phone calls and visits gradually strengthened their friendship. They both realised that they had deep feelings for each other. Jenny was waiting for Alfred to propose. He, on the other hand assumed they were courting. After Jenny had waited in vain for Alfred's proposal for nearly three years of friendship, she said yes to Mike's proposal and told Alfred of her intentions to marry Mike. Alfred felt very cheated, hurt, and heartbroken. He thought of Jenny as a heartless lady who had no emotions and he vowed never to have anything to do with women.

Who do you blame in this instance? Alfred assumed from their closeness that they were courting but Jenny did not. It will be very painful when something precious is snatched from you because you were not bold enough to declare your intentions. Some may argue that Jenny could also have proposed. Yes, there is nothing wrong with a woman proposing if she finds it appropriate. It is not a sin or wrong for a woman to ask a man who keeps hanging around her, "will you marry me"? A woman may prefer this act of boldness and get the man of her heart or refuse to ask the question and loose him to another woman.Be sure of the path you wish to take so that you do not spend your life reciting *"had I known"*. When you are genuinely in love and after diligent prayer where you are convinced that he or she is the right person, don't be intimidated or make assumptions; *Go for his or her love.* You will be happy you did. Certain opportunities come but once. I don't know how it would have been if I had let go of my husband. *He is simply sweet. Don't let another person take what belongs to you.*

This also is not to say that you should propose in haste once you have gathered the facts, as this maymisfire woefully.

I strongly believe that the marriage that will survive begins with friendship. If the friendship is thriving and your potential spouse is happy and satisfied with it, theywill be praying and yearning for more. This means that they will be willing to take you further into courtship and marriage. Some people are tight lipped; they are unnatural and uninteresting. They just meet the person and in their haste, quickly release the bombshell, which, can obviously result in a devastating response. Be timely, remember Ecclesiastes 3:1 clearly states:

"There is a time for everything, and a season for every activity under heaven."

You are also advised not to assume too quickly that a person is in love with you. You might be right but don't rush it, as this conclusion might make you turn away a potentially good relationship if you think you don't love them. True love usually comes out of a developed friendship. Love at first sight can be very dangerous and might be very hurtful if you come to know the truecharacter of the person. Don't judge people until you know them well.

DATING – AN APPOINTMENT THAT DETERMINES THE ALLIGNMENT

Dating is a word we are all familiar with. In one way or the other, we have all dated or been dated at least once in our lifetime. It is more common amongst the youth and until recently, was more European than African. What is dating? When should one date and how many times should it be? What are the dos and don'ts of dating? These are a few of the questions we will be addressing. The Collins Concise Dictionary and Thesaurus defines dating as an appointment, especially with a person of the opposite sex.

Dating is sometimes referred to as a "pre-courtship" meeting of prospective partners, which means that it precedes courtship. It could also be described as taking a prospective partner to a place where you can have some privacy and get to know each other better. Some of the examples are going out for dinner, an excursion, or to places of tourist interest. It is the beginning of friendship and a period of getting to know each other. From here, one can decide whether to go ahead and propose to a person or not. Remember that courtship begins only after proposal and acceptance.

What answer would you give to your ten-year-old brother who asks you about the appropriate time to date? The world has become so complex a place that there are no longer specific times for certain things. In the olden days, there were times to sow and times to reap according to the seasons. Things are however a bit different these days because of technological advancement. As much as we follow scripture, let us also recognise the changes taking place in the world. Nowadays, one can comfortably grow maize in the dry season, thanks to irrigation. In Israel, people use the top of their roofs for gardening. The times for hard and fast rules are over, and the earlier we recognise this, the better it will be for us. The scripture says *watch* the changes taking place in the world in which you live and *pray* according to what you see. Let us not just pray lest we pray amiss.

Saying that the world has become complex however doesn't mean it has become chaotic. There is still law and order in our world as long as the sun rises from the east and sets in the west, let us try to be orderly. Certain necessary conditions must definitely be met before one can think of dating. Some of these are: one's financial position, the intention to marry and the preparedness to do so in the shortest possible time.

FINANCIAL INDEPENDENCE

This means that one should not go dating when he is still being fed from his mother's kitchen and is not in the process of finding a job. This condition however does not apply to those in tertiary institutions. They are usually expected to either gain employment or at least go on a job search after graduating. Actually, I think that the best time to go dating is at the tertiary level of education if one is not working already. Thus you can only go dating when you are financially independent or just about to be. Don't forget that dating may cost money and it will be inappropriate to transfer this cost as an additional cost to your parents. Dating for that matter is not for kids. It is for men.

The Lord God said, "It is not good for the man to be alone. I will make a helper suitable for him." – Gen. 2:18

Many brothers misquote this scripture to their own doom when they declare themselves men and go chasing women. A man is not just an adult male and maturity does not come by the accumulation of years. It only comes about by the acceptance of responsibility, which includes financial independence. Count the cost of dating and be sure that you can financeit before you begin to put undue pressure on your parents.

For which of you, intending to build a tower, sitteth not down first, and counteth the cost, whether he have sufficient to finish it? – Luke 14:28

Another factor to consider before dating is one's intention to marry. Do you really intend to marry the person whom you are dating? Are you just taking her out hoping to get her in bed because she is beautiful to look upon? Are you following that man because of his money or for a night at an expensive hotel? Your commitment to a proper relationship should be the only objective.

Is God happy with the reason why you are going out with that person? Watch out!

Do not gaze at wine when it is red, when it sparkles in the cup, when it goes down smoothly! In the end it bites like a snake and poisons like a viper. – Prov. 23:31-32

Do not follow awoman just because she looks charming. How irresponsible it is to follow a man just because he looks rich. If their intentions for you are not good, you will be sorry in the end.

TIME

Time is another factor that people should consider seriously when going into a relationship. When do you intend to marry should the person say yes to your proposal now? Do you have a set time by which you would like to marry or are you just flowing and waiting for an opportunity? Remember that this opportunity may never come. Dating should be for serious people who intend to marry at a set time, not opportunists who go by the wind. Women should ask men about when they intend to marry before they say yes to them, as some men have wasted women's time in unscheduled relationships which finally fell apart just because there was no planning or the man found a "better" person after years of courtship.

Do not arouse or awaken love until it so desires. –Song. 2:7

Do not talk about dating and courtship until you really mean it and are planning to marry within a specified period of time. Don't deceive a faithful person into following you with all his or her heart when you don't have any genuine plan for marriage. It hurts. If it is just friendship you want, let them understand this ahead of time so that they don't waste their time on you. Don't forget that human beings grow older and not younger as the days go by.

One thing I observed in my lovely relationship with Selgelia was that our vision of marriage kept us from straying away during the trying moments of our love. Beware of the person who is not sure about when he intends to marry you or is not so passionate about marriage. I am not talking about setting wedding dates. The passion with which one makes reasonable efforts to achieve the goal is most important. Set a marital goal and work towards it.

There is no law that states how many times one can date a person before proposing. It depends on how much information one has gathered and the conclusions one has drawn. You must however be careful not to go in too early and watch also, not to be too late. The right time might probably be when the other person is leading you on at a time when you are sure you want it. An Akan saying goes "if you wait for the roasted meat to cool, it may end up cooling in someone else's mouth". Just be on the alert and move strategically.

DATING RESTRICTIONS

One of the most uneasy or even stressful moments in a man's life is the first day out with a woman with whom he is in love. I say this as a man but Selgelia says the women are equally tensed as they try their best in order to impress their date. Who knows?

There are many ways in which potential couples meet for the first time before they arrange a date. This could be on a bus, in school, at Church or at a gospel program. It could also be at a conference or even at a funeral. It could also be arranged on the phone or through the internet when the parties have never met physically. In these days of the internet, people get into various chat rooms and before they realise it, they are falling in love. A friend may also arrange for a date on one's behalf.

No matter where people meet for the first time, a first date is never a comfortable time for any person. First of all, you may never know the likes and dislikes of the other person. You might not be sure whether your date likes with your outfit. You might also not know what conversation will either interest them or put them off. One thing that makes it more uncomfortable is the fact that there might be a hidden agenda, which must be kept tightly sealed until the appointed time. This may result in unnecessary and uninteresting topics for discussion, which may finally earn you an honours degree in boredom. One may therefore ask about what is expected of a man on a first date with the woman whom he loves.

A man is usually expected to call for a date and for that matter, to pay the bills. There is nothing wrong with a woman calling for a date either. You must be very sure that your pocket meets the costs of wherever you plan to go. You must also be prepared to spend a little over the budget. This is what we call "unforeseen circumstances". You must however, not feel shy to ask for support if you run out of cash as a result of unbudgeted expenditure.

Courtesy also demands that the man treats the woman as a queen. This will require services like opening doors for her, pulling out chairs for her and serving her at the table. The man will have to prove that he is capable of taking care of a woman. This will be shown in his gentleness towards her and how self composed he is, not in his bragging and unnecessary display of wealth. Watch out; a braggart is rather a vain man who in reality has nothing to offer a woman. Man, relax and be yourself; you have to be natural because an artificial attitude can mar the whole date. You may however consider being cautious and sensitive. Being humorous can make it interesting but be careful not to become a clown. It becomes boring when it goes beyond some level. After the date, the man is expected to ensure that the woman is safely back at home or at least is on her way home. It is courteous to call later to find out if she arrived safely.

Be careful not to do anything that suggests sex or intimacy. Never on a date should a person force or entice the other for sex. Thou shall not touch, hold, fondle, kiss or peg your date. You should also not allow them to do so to you. Be thou also careful of gazes that can daze. Look elsewhere if the gaze is too sharp and hypnotising. This can be the beginning of danger. Don't allow a date to travel too deep into the night. It is not ideal. Also, privacy is indeed important for a date but obscure locations must be avoided.

As a woman, you are expected to be courteous, polite and lady-like. Appreciate his efforts with a thank you. Dress modestly and decently as a woman. How loud is your lipstick? Contribute to the fun at the date by responding; starting it yourself will not be bad either. Being a clown is however not advisable. Be careful not to be too demanding. You can also decline some offers if you think they are too expensive. A date is not supposed to ruin one's bank account. Avoid doing anything that suggests sex and also be on the alert for date rape. Be sure there is an escape route at the place of the date and also be sure of how you will defend yourself in case there is an attack. Avoid alcohol and any drink that you are unsure of. Make sure that a parent or a friend is aware of everything about the date and try to stick to the original plan.

Also, beware of the information you divulge about yourself. It could make you vulnerable. Being too careful might also stifle the flow. Discretion must be used.

You may also consider contributing to the financing of the date if the situation demands it. After all you never went in to suck them dry, did you? Petting and other romantic games should be avoided. Finally, remember to say thank you when all is over and don't forget to call when you get home. Enjoy your date, I hope it develops into a fruitful marriage; remember that it can be stressful, demanding and risky as well as rewarding and satisfying.

Whatever the situation, do not be afraid. Know that the Lord is with you and will not let you dash your feet against the stones of life if you walk according to His statutes. Feel free, enjoy yourself and be sure that your date is a fruitful one. Remember however that you will be required to give account of everything you do with your youthful days in two ways. With God on the judgment day, and also to your matured self when you grow old. Life is shorter than it seems to you now. Don't waste it in your youthful days. Today is the foundation for tomorrow. Build it well with carefully guided decisions, which consider genuineness rather than charm and vainglory. Take time to invest into your future by studying hard, working hard, saving some money, associating with the right people and praying strategically and prophetically into your life. God will do the rest. See you at the top when we get there. God bless you.

THE COURTSHIP THAT LEADS TO MARRIAGE

Courtship can be defined by the Collins Dictionary as the act of making oneself open to an intended spouse or mate. It is usually the period between the time of proposal acceptance and marriage. It is a period of decision for marriage or against marriage hence it has to be treated with utmost seriousness. Efforts should be made to have a successful courtship. Remember that your input determines your output. However, it is not all courtships that lead to marriage. Prayer, carefulness, selflessness, sacrifice, love and sharing of quality time are necessary for effective courtship that leads to marriage. Certain basic qualities needed in marriage are also important in courtship. This is not to say that courtship is marriage but it is a very important step towards marriage.

Some of the very basic ingredients that contribute to the success or otherwise of a relationship are: communication, sacrifice, trust, spirituality, forgiveness, focus and the influence of other relevant people. Besides these, is the most important element without which, no relationship will ever see success. This element is *agreement.* It is clearly asked in Amos 3:3:

"Do two walk together unless they have agreed to do so?"

Have you proposed to the woman you love? Have you accepted a proposal from the man you love? Have you two agreed on certain terms and conditions upon which the relationship should be based? Are you convinced that you agree with this newfound love without reservations? God bless you. You have started a journey, which could be the beginning of a responsible and fulfilling life. You must now determine never to let this new relationship lead you to sorrow. It is a double-edged sword that you now have in your hands. It can bring you immeasurable joy as well as unfathomable pain and disappointment. As a child of God, the power is in your hands for the determination of your marital future.

Be assured that there are lots of surprises, both good and bad in this new way of life. It is a very exciting time but you can make it very boring if you do not handle it well. It is my heartfelt prayer that the Good Lord goes with you as you move on in faith to fulfil your blessed destiny. Be bold and strong because although the journey can sometimes be tough, the Lord your God will always be there for you. You must now learn to say, “I love you”.

CHAPTER 12

COMMUNICATION

THE WILL-FORCE OF WORDS

Communication may be defined as the exchange of information, ideas or feelings by speech, writing or other means. It is the expression of one's feelings, intensions and experiences to another person or other people. These feelings and intentions are encoded in speech, gestures, music and facial expressions among others by the communicator. The recipient of the information is expected to decode its meaning with a relatively high level of accuracy in order to make the communication valid. In other words, for communication to be valid, the recipient should understand the information being passed on to him or her. Communication is thus said never to be complete until the recipient fully understands it. Therefore, if you are sent an important message, which has been written in Chinese when you don't understand it, there has not been effective communication.

Man is said to be gregarious or social, which means that no man survives on his own. Everyone needs the company of others no matter how rich, spiritual, educated, beautiful or powerful they may be. However, for this social co-existence to be possible there is the need for communication. The Bible says, "two cannot walk together unless they agree". Agreement also, can never be possible without communication. In actual fact, wherever two or more people are expected to do anything together successfully, there is the need for effective communication. In Business Studies, communication is said to be the nerve centre of every organisation. In Biology, the nervous system is defined as "the brain, spinal column, and nerves which together control thought, feeling and movement". Thus without the nerves, man cannot live. In the same way, two cannot do anything together without communication. When communication is poisoned, relationships are destroyed. This is why the Bible says in 1 Corinthians 15:33:

"Be not deceived: evil communications corrupt good manners."

Effective communication is therefore vital to the success of every courtship. Most problems can be solved and better still avoided when prospective partners know what to say at what time to each other. Through communication, the real personality of the person is revealed; one gets to know the likes and dislikes of the other party, which helps to reduce or prevent unnecessary arguments and statements that could cause hurt.

Constructive criticisms should be made where the need arises in every courtship. This however should be communicated clearly and effectively so as to avoid misinterpretation. The reason for the criticism should be to correct as well as the language. Rebuke to teach, not to condemn.

Communication was a problem I had with Derek, given that I was born and bred in Accra as a Ga whilst he has a very divergent background as a Fante who has lived and travelled in many parts of Ghana and the world, and our statements always meant something else to the other person. I did not appreciate his sense of politeness whereas he easily got offended with almost every statement that I made. He felt that I was rude and I also felt that he was too critical. I easily got fed up with him since he would not let any statement go uncriticised. In this area, our diverse backgrounds contributed to our inability to communicate with each other in an effective way. The frustration was so intense at times that I considered backing out from the relationship. However, God knew what he was doing and saw us through successfully. If you happen to be in a similar situation, do not give up, just acknowledge the problem and understand that this particular issue takes time to heal.

In this Chapter, we will take time to discuss some of the issues, which creates communication problems in our day-to-day intercourse with our dear ones as well as other people. Take good notes of these issues, and determine in your mind that they will notcause your relationship to disintegrate.

I AM HURT!

Wherever two individuals live in harmony, there are also offences. Sociologists will tell you that conflict is a necessary ingredient for unity, which leads to progress. Where there are no offences, there is retrogression. Offences also rejuvenate relationships and make everything start afresh. Our problem now is how do we communicate our hurts to our partners? There are many ways in which people express their dissatisfaction. Some of these expressions are crying, shouting abuses, cursing, going out, shirking responsibility and going “dumb”. Which of these do you usually do?

Yes it is very true that your partner was very wrong to have done what they did but have you ever been told that courtship and marriage are not for babies? They are for matured people who are bold enough to handle serious offences without going mad. It is emotionally very helpful to express hurt but always remember that reason will have to precede emotions. The Bible says in Proverbs 16:32 that:

"He that is slow to anger is better than the mighty; and he that ruleth his spirit than he that taketh a city."

Controlling your emotions is necessary if you hope to get anywhere with that man or woman. Crying may relieve you of the tension but don't make a nuisance out of it since it could lead to more hurt if it irritates your partner. Crying in isolation is always better than doing it for people to see. It clearly defines your baby nature. Don't forget that we all cry when the going gets tough, however it depends on how you do it.

Cursing and shouting abusive words should not at any time be part of our bid to get our feelings across. The fact that you are in a relationship does not negate your allegiance to Christ who died for you, God your father who is looking after you and the Holy Spirit who lives in you as a witness to your salvation. You are still a Christian.

Bless them, which persecute you; bless and curse not. –Rom. 12:14

Never let profanity out of your holy mouth because someone offended you. Never use abusive words because you feel that you have reasons to do so.

But I say unto you, that whosoever is angry of his brother without a cause shall be in danger of the judgment: and whosoever shall say unto his brother, Raca, shall be in danger of the council: but whosoever shall say, Thou fool, shall be danger of hellfire. –Matt. 5:22

On this note I would urge you to rule your spirit and save your soul from hellfire.

Shirking of responsibility and going dumb should not be a form of making your hurt known. In so doing, you may end up creating more problems for your partner and yourself. Emotions are different from reason. It is always better to use your mind in times of problems than to use your heart.

Miriam also decided to go dumb after her husband had chosen that method for days after a misunderstanding. Her husband, Davy, had a promotion interview to attend. He decided to sleep a little before the interview. He wrote on a sheet of paper "wake me up at 2:00 o'clock". When it was time, Miriam also wrote on a sheet of paper "it is 2:00o'clock, wake up".

You can guess what happened next. Miriam could also have overlooked her husband's misbehaviour for the common good of the family. The promotion was not only for Davy but also for the whole family. What do we gain when we decide to repay our partners for something they have done wrong? There is nothing as beautiful as forgiving a partner who has hurt you. The one who is able to control their emotions and go about offences in a sensible manner is called a *wise person.* Imagine how you will feel if you loose a cherished one because you cursed, insulted or slapped them.

What will you do if after having left home in anger you were involved in an accident? This does not imply that we are not justified in getting angry, as anger is a part of life and even the Bible allows it BUT how you go about it is important. In Ephesians 4:26, the Bible declares:

"Be ye angry, and sin not: let not the sun go down on your wrath."

I know and understand how painful and frustrating it is when you are hurt by the person whom you trust and love so much, but brethren let us allow the word of God to take control of our emotions so that we can do the right thing when we are hurt or angered. Release the notion that you have to be apologised to before you forgive. We may never know how much we have offended God and not apologised but does He hold them against us? Which of us will survive without His love and forgiveness?

The above statement not only apply to the offended but to the offender, the Bible says that we should do everything possible to live in peace with all men. It is obligatory therefore for you to say sorry even if you think that you are not wrong, for Christ's sake. Let us learn to control our anger and to forgive without demanding an apology. In the same way, let us learn to apologise instead of justifying our offences.

He who covers an offense promotes love, but whoever repeats the matter separates close friends. –Prov. 17:9

My husband always says, "*there is a better way of going about everything.*" Let us therefore choose the better way and remember that love is not easily angered and keeps no record of wrong. One may ask at this juncture, which way is better? Instead of reacting in such a way that will make things worse or make you regret your actions when everything is over, why don't you try and tell your partner calmly; "darling I am hurt by what you said". The offender will also do great good if they learn to say, "oh sweetheart, I'm sorry, I did not intend to offend you but this was what I meant. However I'm still sorry". Keep in mind also that arguing is a leading cause of broken relationships. Instead of insisting on what you think is right at the expense of your partner, why don't you just give in or denounce a single conviction so that your relationship can survive. May God bless you as you learn to control your anger as well as learn to say sorry.

As much as we are talking about controlling anger, partners should also make a conscious effort not to hurt each other and should be quick to apologise when the need arises. You decided to court your partner because you love and hold themin high regard above all others; therefore there is the need for you to be careful in relating to your loved one. Reducing offences and hurts as much as possible strengthens the relationship. The choice of words when communicating with each other is very important. It can either cause a lot of problems or make the relationship a lovely one.

Proverbs 16:24 says that:

"Pleasant words are a honeycomb, sweet to the soul and healing to the bones."

We have to learn to use the right words at the right time if we want to reduce offences and make our relationship rich and enjoyable. Unfortunately, some of us do not know how to "speak". The good news is that we can always learn. Make every effort to know your partner and how to reach him or her with the right words. The Bible says in Proverbs 15:1:

"A soft answer turneth away wrath: but grievous words stir up anger".

I AM SORRY

I will arise and go to my father, and will say unto him, Father, I have sinned against heaven, and before thee, And am no more worthy to be called thy son: make me as one of thy hired servants. And he arose, and came to his father. But when he was yet a great way off, his father saw him, and had compassion, and ran, and fell on his neck, and kissed him. – Luke 15:18-20

Humility is the bedrock of every successful relationship including marriage. It is a sign of wisdom. As simple as the word sorry may seem, it goes a very long way. The prodigal son was able to regain his place in his father's heart because he had the wisdom to say sorry. You will also find a way back into your partner's heart if you know how to say sorry. Never find it hard to say "sorry" even when you do not see the imminent need to. Never struggle to say it when you see your spouse is hurt even when they have not communicated their feelings of unhappiness.

And when Abigail saw David, she hasted, and lighted off the ass, and fell before David on her face, and bowed herself to the ground, And fell at his feet, and said, Upon me, my lord, upon me let this iniquity be: and let thine handmaid, I pray thee, speak in thine audience, and hear the words of thine handmaid. – 1 Sam. 25:23-24

Learn to say sorryoften; say it when you're late for an appointment or a date, say it when you have said something you shouldn't have said. Say it when you sense your partner is disappointed. Say it when you cannot meet a certain expectation. Just learn to say sorry without giving any unnecessary justifications. Your partner is moved more by the brokenness of your spirit than the proud justification of your actions. You will lose nothing for being apologetic in your demeanour. Say sorry and mean it. Your partner will know it if you are only saying it for saying sake. Have a heart that is humble and wise. Abigail changed from being the wife of a fool to being the wife of a King through her ability to say SORRY.

And when David heard that Nabal was dead, he said, Blessed be the LORD, ...And David sent and communed with Abigail, to take her to him to wife. –1 Sam. 25:39

I LOVE YOU

This 4-letter word "*love*" is very controversial especially in Christian relationships. Is it wrong to talk about love as a Christian when one is still not married? It was my biggest problem at the beginning of my relationship with Derek. I felt it was a sin and was very careful not to say it. I love you could mean a lot of things to different groups of people. What does it mean to you? Do we however have enough reason for not expressing love to the ones we love? This makes us hypocrites because we are actually practicing that which we think is a sin to talk about. You are already in a love relationship but fear to talk about love. My personal point of view in this case is that, it is not a sin for a matured person who is courting a loved one for marriage to say I love you.

People are also very careful with this issue of love because of cultural prohibitions. In many cultures, it is considered immoral for a woman to propose to a man. This ideology transcends into courtship and even marriage. Women are somehow forbidden from expressing their feelings towards men. They are considered immoral for expressing genuine feelings. That perception is however fast fading with the onset of modernisation. Women should therefore have no excuse for not expressing love. There is not a single scripture that forbids women from saying "I love you".

It is true that lovers should understand that their partners would not continue with the relationship if they no longer loved them. However, the most satisfying words a person expects from a loved one would be "I love you". Do you realise that you like talking about things you love? For example, a man might continue talking about his new car for a whole year, still recognising it as new. A woman may also keep on admiring a newly born baby for years. On the other hand we hate remembering or being reminded of nasty incidences or things that we hate. Lovers should therefore make it a point to express their love to their partners without any reservations irrespective of their sex.

One must however be cautious when expressing love. The world usually interprets love as sex. Expressing love therefore may bring to mind sex and romance which if not well handled, could lead to fornication. Sex is a way of expressing love but that is only within the context of marriage. One cannot express love through extra marital-sex and still remain righteous or holy. Women especially should be careful of the deception that men bring their way "if you love me why don't you want us to have sex?" Some may deceitfully settle for romance. Don't forget that romance is a sure ticket to sex. A man by asking for your love expression may only be asking for romance but be warned; he is thinking of sex as the final objective. You may only end up picking the pieces from sexual immorality. Don't start it! If your partner does not understand that love outside marriage has limitations, they are not good enough for marriage. Let them go. You may ask me now "but I love him?" The only answer I have for you is this "do not love any man more than God and also if they leave you, God will continue loving you until the right man comes your way. I have been there and I tell you to stay away because the possible consequences are too nasty and unbearable. Your world might just come to an end.

Watch out. You don't want to get pregnant before marriage as a Christian. Do you? You may not want to hide the pregnancy and commit abortion, which could lead to death, barrenness and even give you sexually transmitted diseases including HIV-AIDS. Would you? Don't forget that this same man who is fighting for your sex-love may not be able to stand with you when the pressure is tough. He may end up leaving you to your fate *when the seed bears fruit.* Love is good and expressing love is great. However, please wait until you are married before you experiment or play with your bodies. In spite of the fact that this idea is scriptural, it is also absolutely common sense. Think and act wisely as a Christian so as not to bring shame to yourself and God. Be careful not to rush because when you marry, you may not even have the strength and time for all that you have been craving. I have been there. In marriage, you do it in absolute dignity and with a free mind. God richly bless you as you decide to wait until you are married before you go all out.

HOW DO I LOOK?

Not too long ago, Selgelia asked me on our way out to the market: "how am I looking?" This answer was not pre-meditated but I found myself saying "like a monkey". The only good thing about this answer was that she kept chasing me till we got to the bus stop, just in time for the bus. I only escaped with that because we were in a very romantic mood and so there was no room for animosity.

People, especially women like to be complimented by their loved ones when they are well dressed. It is not as if they can't see that they are looking good but it serves as some form of reassurance of love from the man they love. A woman feels "yea he is still mad about me, he loves me, he thinks I'm more beautiful than the other ladies". She feels "the good comments mean that he would want me to stay on for as long as time will permit". Psychologically, she gets the feeling that her contract with you has been renewed any time you praise her. Do you know that every employee who gets the assurance that his or her contract is being renewed puts up his or her best? This means that you stand a chance of getting your partner to do great in the relationship as you keep on assuring her of her beauty, sense of dressing and your total commitment to her.

Unfortunately, some men are quite poor when it comes to praising their women to an extent that even when they are asked the question which I failed, they fail too. What would you say if your, darling after waiting so long for your compliment without any success, ask you: "how am I looking?" Will you tell her "well I was just waiting for us to get out there, then I would beg you never to leave me because you are the most beautifully dressed woman I have ever seen" or would you do as most men do and say "you are alright, hurry up before we are late" or worse still "you remind me of this nightmare". Let us get the message right. She actually asked you "do you really love me just this way that I look or do you have any reservations about me?" Be fast and respond appropriately before it costs you your love.

I have heard of stories when women have been snatched from their loved ones or even husbands because of the words used. If there is one thing that I like about the Ashantis of Ghana, it will be their choice of words, especially for women. They refer to all women as "Ohemaa" meaning queen. She may be well aware that she is not a queen but those sweet words will definitely make her comfortable in her dealings with you. She will feel at home and will love you more.

Women should also complimenttheir men on the way they are dressed. Way back in university, if there was anything that Selgelia did to make me feel better, it was her comments about my dressing at least on Sundays. I was worship leader and I thank God for that. Before I would leave my room each Sunday morning, Selgelia would come up and help me with preparations after which she would take a careful look at me and say "you are looking great". I thank God for His anointing upon my life but that comment was also a great boost at least psychologically for a good praise session. I would stand before the congregation and only concentrate on God because Selgelia says my dressing is excellent. I did not care about whatever other people would think about my appearance. You know what, comments of such nature are very important. A poor description of how I was looking could have sent me raising warfare songs for worship. Ladies and gentlemen, this love business is all about commitment, faithfulness, appreciation and praises. Ignore the flat nose and compliment the long hair. God bless you.

HOW AM I DOING?

One uncomfortable situation in a relationship is to feel that your partner does not appreciate you beyond the basics. How would you feel if you never get an extra commendation apart from the usual ritualistic 'thank you'? Your partner would be happier if you could just sit them down one evening and talk about all the good things they do and how you could not do without their support. In the first place, it is a sign of humility, which is an important ingredient for a successful relationship. It also gives your partner reason not to doubt his or her value in the relationship. Funny enough, we realise the importance of our loved ones often after they are gone. This is not a good experience! Avoid it! Someone said "had I known is always the philosophy of the unwise". If your man is responsible, let him know he is. Perhaps he would do it more. If your woman is hard-working, tell her. She may begin to also improve on her spending style.

Before I forget, let us remember that many people fail to give good comments because they are looking elsewhere at this lady or gentleman who is so good at something else. They could focus on this imaginary person who looks great from afar to the point of thinking that their partner may be good for nothing. Don't be fooled, you will only know what they really are, after you get close to them. Don't forget that you may never have them if they really are that good. One elderly man once told me "it is our short comings that cause us to be paired with such imperfect people". In other words, he means that before you put away that imperfect person, take an unbiased look at yourself. You may end up being grateful for having them. Take a good look at your head, teeth, legs, nose, eyes, height, hair, education, social background, and even your voice. There, you will realise that God needs to be praised for giving you such a partner.

MISSING YOU

Does your partner miss you when you are not around? If your answer is yes, there must be a reason and if no, there is also a reason. How can one forget about a partner whose speech is full of motivation, encouragement, inspiration, appreciation and hope? The Bible says in Isaiah 52:7:

"*How beautiful on the mountains are the feet of those who bring good news, who proclaim peace, who bring good tidings, who proclaim salvation, who say to Zion, "Your God reigns!""*

Taking a critical look at this scripture, you can see that the feet of the bearer of good news is the first part of the body to be praised. If even the feet are being praised, what do you think will be said of the face? Motivators, peaceful people and humourists are so precious to those who come into contact with them that their absence is easily felt. Can the same be said of you? There are some people whose absence brings joy and relief to their partners because their presence brings depression, sorrow, helplessness, hopelessness and frustration.

It is all in communication. How do you talk? Do you talk as if you own the American continent? Do you make people feel inferior with your words? Some Christian men brag about everything including spirituality. They make you feel like a sinner immediately as you come into their presence. Their statements are full of condemnation of others while they brag about how they are making it in the Kingdom. It is demonic. These people do not radiate the true presence of the Holy Spirit. Don't forget that some people are in the Church for their own selfish ambitions. Don't fall prey to them. They are the kind of people who you remember and your heart starts to beat faster and you start to sweat for no apparent reason. You start to think and you realise that you are dealing with an evil man even if he thinks that he is a bishop.

There are some other people whose presence brings healing. They are full of true praises and motivation. They urge you on. They never call any situation, hopeless because they know what God can do. They never condemn people because they know where they are coming from. They hardly brag because they recognise God as the source of all good things. They talk about the future with reference to the will of God. Finally, they have some amount of humour to cheer you up for the day. Do you know that there are some people whom you remember and you start laughing? They make your heart joyful and that is good medicine for your soul. They really bring healing.

A man's spirit sustains him in sickness, but a crushed spirit who can bear? –Prov.18:14

Do not hang around people who will dampen your spirit!

Talking about wanting to be with some people more than others also brings to mind a friend who is popularly known as "*talking sense*". Some people seem not to have any reasonable contribution to a topic but they surely have to talk about almost everything. The Bible says that even the fool, when he keeps quiet, is considered as being wise (Proverbs 17:28).

For godly and sensible people to like your utterances, they must be seasoned with salt, inspiring, interesting, motivating and balanced. Are your deliberations and decisions word based. Just to remind you, this virtue does not come by magic, but by continuous study of scripture and applying it to real life in wisdom as the spirit leads you.

This book of the law shall not depart out of your mouth; but you shall meditate therein day and night, that you may observe to do according to all that is written therein: for then thou shall make thy way prosperous, and then thou shall have good success. – Josh. 1:8

When you see a decent man who is loved and wanted by all level headed people, do not think that he just happens to be like that. It comes from so much sacrifice and laborious study, which is rightly crowned by the anointing. Desire the things of God and be ready to sacrifice for it and you too will be desired. You cannot live carelessly and still carry the attracting anointing.

CHAPTER 13

SHOW INTEREST

How interested are you in the topic being raised by your partner? Is it boring? Doesn't make any sense? You may be right. We all have different backgrounds and aspirations. These reflect on our modes of thinking and the things that interest us. A person who has had a medical practitioner for a parent and aspires to be a doctor will definitely be more interested in medical and scientific issues. On the other hand, a business-oriented person will be thinking about the stock exchange, inflation and taxation.

In the situation where two people with different interests fall in love, one may not always be interested in what interests the other. Biologically, women have quite a more complex body than men have. Their feelings at particular times may also differ. They may tend to complain about things that mean little to a man. The same also applies to the introvert and the extrovert. They have opposing interests. And the list could go on.

The Bible also says that *two cannot walk together unless they agree*. This means that there must be a *no man's land* in your conversations where individual interests are put aside for general issues that can be discussed comfortably. Issues like sports, politics, travelling and child-care could comfortably be dealt with. The topic doesn't always need to be what interests you most before you give it your attention. The family cannot be built without communication. You have to talk extensively on many issues as the days go by and you are obliged to take interest and to contribute. Building a fortified family demands no less dedication.

There are times when you will not want to talk about a particular issue but if that is what they want, why not give it some time. You may even end up getting interested as time goes on. In marriage, there are no women issues or men issues. Every little issue is equally important. Give it time and let your partner feel at home. Everybody wants to communicate his or her feelings. Give your partner the attention that you will need some time later. You know that you feel bad when you don't get the response that you expect. Don't let your partner feel the same way. Give them time and attention. Show some interest and it will certainly come back to you.

You will do yourself and your partner some good if you don't feign sleep or actually start to doze off when they are talking about something. Contributing as well as giving a few reasonable responses will make them feel good. You must however take care not to *hijack* the conversation to your own advantage. There are many instances where people have taken over the conversation and given a full lecture, usually about their own selves. This attitude is very bad. It makes you boring. It is a sign of selfishness and disregard for the other person's level of intelligence. Do not forget also, to give reasonable answers when you are asked questions that even seem to irritate you. Do not let your answers to questions give room for your partner to doubt you.

As we talk about showing interest in conversations, we are also talking about the foundations of our discussions. We have to endeavour to season our communication with true salt bearing in mind that only the house that is built on the rock will withstand the stormy weather. Before making any comment, let us ask ourselves if it will be pleasing to the Lord. This is the surest secret to a peaceful and uplifting conversation.

THE RIGHT-WAY TO ASK

There are some questions that sound so rude and demeaning that you may not want to answer them. Let's take these examples. A friend visits you and you want to cook. What is the best question to ask in order to find out if they would want to take part in the meal? Which of these two would you want to be asked? "Johnny,

I am cooking some rice for you. I hope you will like it or would you prefer potatoes instead?"Or "Johnny I am cooking some rice. Will you eat?"A sensitive person will definitely answer in the negative. You have to make every effort to ensure that your questions are very inviting and appetising if you want your guests and loved ones to joyfully get involved in your programs.

Favours have to be asked in all humility. Some people are so rude that they never get what they ask for. They ask for favours as if they were insisting on their rights. You will not get what you want if you don't know how to ask in humility. Humility does not cheapen you before your partner; it rather puts you in a position to be helped. You end up getting what you ask for and even more than you ask. You get what you want when you are able to appeal to people's conscience. Asking for favours in humility will not change anything about you. In fact, you will loose nothing. Why don't you therefore choose the appropriate words? Ask in humility and get what you want rather than loose what you want because of pride. You could consider "could you please help me with this…" rather than asking "will you do that for me?".

COMMENTS

Watch your thoughts, because they become words, which in turn become actions, which form a habit and develop into a character which ultimately leads to your destiny.

Finally, brethren, whatsoever things are true, whatsoever things are honest, whatsoever things are just, whatsoever things are pure, whatsoever things are lovely, whatsoever things are of good report, if there be any virtue, and if there be any praise, think of these things. – Phil. 4:8

For as he thinketh in his heart, so is he. – Prov. 23:7a

A word fitly spoken is like apples of gold in pictures of silver. – Prov. 25:11

A comment, it is said, could be more devastating than an atomic bomb. It could also be as soothing as a healing balm. Your comments on issues can go a long way to affect your partner in one way or the other. Women, as already discussed are seriously moved by comments because they are more emotional and sensitive. We have to be as careful as possible when making comments to our loved ones. If a loved one is hurt or not comfortable with certain comments, do you still have to continue making them? Most of us intentionally or unintentionally make certain comments concerning tribes, size, nose, legs, style of walking, former school and the list goes on and on. A person who has said yes to your proposal has also gone all the way to somehow entrusting their life into your hands. They believe and trust that you will handle them with care and dignity. I am very sure that you saw and liked the nose of your fiancée before proposing. Do you think they will be happy when you continue reminding them of that odd thing? What comments do you make when you see other ladies in town as a man in courtship? No human being will want to be made to feel inadequate by other people's comments. Yes it is true you went to "a first class school" while she went to a "third class school" but is your love based on schools attended or that inner quality in your partner? It will be very painful if you always give demeaning comments about your partner. Love is a matter of giving the best of you to your partner. Why should you continue to make those comments when he or she has told you several times or acted in a way for you to know that it hurts? You could easily dampen your partner's spirit with a careless comment. This could go a long way in affecting your partner in a way that could never be healed. I remember that when I was young, my uncle made a comment about a particular part of my body. If it had not been for my husband, I would never have liked that part of my body. I was so hurt that I tried several ways of destroying that part of my body. Surprisingly, it is the part of my body my husband cherishes most. If I was so hurt by someone with whom I was not in love with, imagine the extent to which your negative comments can have on somebody who has given their heart to you. Let us therefore be careful and try to please our partners rather than being selfish and insisting on what we want. I know it is not easy because of the many differences between human beings but all the same, love should make us sacrifice.

You will get what you want when you give what is needed. Don't be making comments that would make your partner feel like they do not mean anything to you. What comments do you make about the opposite sex? Your fiancé may not have a car. What comments do you make about other men with cars? Your partner may not have long hair, how do you make her feel when you see other ladies with long hair? If you want an exciting relationship, you have to know what to say at what time. Love involves a lot of sacrifices. As much as possible, always make your partner feel wanted and loved. Don't push him or her away with your comments. Remember, there is no perfect person and everybody has something odd about them. Focusing on a person's good points and commenting positively will help them to be what you really want them to be. Unfortunately, we forget that some people find themselves in certain unfavourable situations not by any fault of their own. Imagine if you are going on a date with a partner who is from a "poor" background. They may not be well dressed to match your standards. What do you tell such a person when you meet? Do you make derogatory comments about their dressing? Think about the effect a negative comment will have on such a person taking into consideration their background. Life is about making another person feel loved, happy and wanted. Let us make this world a better place for our loved ones.

HONESTY AND SINGLE MINDEDNESS

For he that wavereth is like a wave of the sea driven with the wind and tossed. – Jam. 1:6

Are you hiding anything from your partner for some reason? What reason is it? Why do you hide things from the one you desire to live with for the rest of your life? When secrets begin to flourish in a relationship, godliness begins to die out. Adam and Eve only recognised that they were naked and had to cover themselves after they had sinned and fallen short of the presence of God. Your partner should have no problem with whatever concerns you if it is in God's direction and also if theyare in the same direction. In a partnership where some things have to be hidden, there are two possible reasons. Either the issue is ungodly or either of the party is ungodly. Think about it. No matter what you do, your relationship will suffer if you keep secrets. Even if it is a sin you have committed, do not hide it. Confess it and be forgiven. Do not conceal your sins out of pride. The Bible says that he who conceals his sin does not progress but he who confesses and stops it receives mercy. Confess it, be forgiven and checked before whatever sin it is, destroys you.

He that covereth his sins shall not prosper: but whoso confesseth and forsaketh them shall have mercy. – Prov.28:13

Before we got married, I was in London alone and was tempted with a terrible sin one day. This was a sin that looked good and promised so much of a good future. In spite of this promise it was still a sin. Selgelia was in Ghana and would not have known anything about it. Honesty however did not allow me to take advantage of the situation. I had to call her and give a detailed explanation of my current situation and ask to be prayed for. I had to forget about all the respect that she had for me as a "*boy of God"(the younger version of a man of God)* and face reality. But God is so good and faithful that this openness rather made

Selgelia love and respect me more because she came to the conclusion that there is nothing that I am going to hide from her. Let your partner know wherever you are or may be at every point in time. Let them know and approve of your friends. Build their confidence in you through your single mindedness. Obey your own word. If you promise to be at Church at one o'clock, be there.

But above all things, my brethren, swear not, neither by heaven, neither by the earth, neither by any other oath: but let you yea be yea; and you nay, nay; lest ye fall into condemnation. – Jam. 5:12

Let us be true to ourselves and make the world know that the devil has no claim in our lives. Satan is the father of all liars! Do not say it if you do not mean it. There is no such thing as white lies in heaven. Don't aim togive excuses that contain elements of lies. These may not be seen by anyone but could cost you your eternity in heaven.

THINKING OF TOMMORROW?

He is like a man which built an house, and dug deep, and laid the foundation on a rock: and when the flood arose, the stream beat vehemently upon that house, and could not shake it: for it was founded upon a rock. – Luke 6:48

Many people live as if the world ends at the end of the day. There is nothing wrong with this if you do it in the positive sense, thus staying away from sin with the understanding that Christ may come back at any time. If you however do it negatively by consuming all the good things in your life without sowing any for the future, the Bible likens you to the foolish man in the proverb of Luke 6.

Life is like fire. It needs fuel to burn. If you therefore burn the fuel without any replenishment, the fire may die out. Many people have killed the joy out of their Christian lives by not spending time to fast, pray and study. These are the fuel of a glowing Christian life. Education and or the study of a trade are also the fuel of your future competence in life. Living one's youth without any of these ingredients will simply burn the fuel out of your future happiness. These are matters of reality. You cannot run away from them.

Can you imagine how much time and effort that it took the wise man to dig and build upon the rock? Think of how easy it was for the foolish man to build on the sand. Such is life. The Biblestates in Psalm126:5 that:

"They that sow in tears shall reap in joy."

Son of God, daughter of God, as the Bible refers you, please endure some pain in all aspects of your life if you wish to build something for a better future life. Life has two sides: the positive and the negative. You cannot avoid any of them. You however have a choice as to which of them you want first. You can enjoy your youthful days in laziness and lavishness and endure a painful old age. You can also endure a painful and laborious youthfulness and enjoy a pleasant old age.

This quality will have to be seen in your prospective spouse. Never give in to a man or woman who is not prepared to sacrifice for the future. They cannot sacrifice for you. Let your partner know how much you are putting into your future and how you are preparing for a good and responsible adult life. You must also be sure that they are doing the same thing before you fall for them. Don't fall for a "gay" person who is just blowing their life away even if they seem so popular and appealing. That is how they are at the beginning. They are just spending without earning. Look for them in a few years and they are nowhere to be found. Let your partner trust that you are building a good foundation for your future together.

CHAPTER 14

THE "SHIP" IN COURTSHIP

DON'T CAPSIZE YOUR SHIP!

The moment two people decide to walk together, they intend to share a common destiny. One says to the other, knowingly or otherwise, that, "your God shall be my God and your fate shall be my fate". Two people cannot walk together if they still have separate lives, destinations and aspirations.

Walking together therefore means that you both decide to board the same ship to the same destination whether it is good or bad. Ask yourself, who is the pilot of this ship in which you are both sailing? There are instances where people have both worshiped God faithfully as individuals but have come together and have substituted God with each other. I have experienced it before. If the Lord of host is not piloting the ship in your courtship, how do you plan to sail through the storms? If you are piloting it yourselves, where are you heading for?

Blessed is the nation whose God is the LORD; – Ps. 33:12a

In other words, blessed is the courtship which has the Lord God as its pilot. Do not forget this scripture. Always make sure that God is not stolen from you by way of your entering into courtship.

CREDIT YOUR PRAYER BANK RIGHT NOW!

Then shall the kingdom of heaven be likened unto ten virgins who took their lamps, and went forth to meet the bridegroom. And five of them were wise, and five were foolish. They that were foolish took their lamps, and took no oil with them: But the wise took oil in their vessels with their lamps. While the bridegroom tarried, they all slumbered and slept. And at midnight there was a cry made, Behold, the bridegroom cometh; go ye out to meet him. Then all those virgins arose, and trimmed their lamps. And the foolish said unto the wise, Give us of your oil; for our lamps are gone out. But the wise answered saying, No so; lest there be not enough for us and you: but go ye rather to them that sell, and buy for yourselves. And while they went to buy, the bridegroom came; and they that were ready went in with him to the marriage: and the door was shut. Afterward came also the other virgins, saying Lord, Lord, open to us. But he answered and said, Verily I say unto you, I know you not. – Matt. 25:1-12

The family that prays together, it is said, stays together. If you want your relationship to work well, spend time praying together in advance. This becomes more important when you think of a successful married life. You have to pray a lot into the future. Bank the prayers into your life and future marriage. Even Jesus used this strategy, so why won't you?

And in the morning, rising up a great while before day, he went out, and departed into a solitary place, and there prayed. – Mark 1:35

Jesus knew the importance of praying ahead of time. This is why He would wake up long before the day begins and go out to pray into the day. Learn to pray into your marriage a great while before it is due. Do not limit it only to your marriage but also to all spheres of your life. Pray into your education, profession, family and all other things before they pose problems. Do not wait for the problems to come up before you pray. Let the solutions be born out of prayer, rather than wait for the problems. Do not let them take you by surprise. Be wise. Be like the five wise virgins who anticipated future fuel shortages and made provisions for themselves. Do not wait for Kojo to tell you that it is over between you two before you start to pray. Pray that he would never say it at all.

And the angel of the LORD came again the second time, and touched him, and said, Arise and eat; because the journey is too great for thee. – 1 Kin. 19:7

Child of God, ARISE and pray, for the life ahead of you is too great for you. You cannot possibly survive it without any savings in your prayer bank.

THE WORD – YOUR GUARANTEE FOR A FIRM STANDING

Thy word is a lamp unto my feet, and a light unto my path. – Ps. 119:105

Among all the things I gratefully learnt in the Scripture Union is this memory verse which has truly been a lamp unto my feet and a light unto my path. The path that we are all treading is dark enough to require some amount of lighting and the surest light that one can ever get is the light of God. Let the word of God penetrate into the deepest crevices of your relationship, let it season your relationship and preserve it in these evil days.

Hide the word of God in your individual hearts and play scriptural games to help you remember quotations. You will be amazed how beneficial they will be to you in times of trouble. Build your relationship on the surest rock, Jesus who is also the word. As long as the sun rises in the east and sets in the west, problems will come to mortal men at various times. All men face problems but not all men come out the same. The difference is in the word. The word of God will break every rock that stands in your way. However, this will only happen if the word is in your heart and you know how to use it appropriately.

Is not my word like fire" declares the Lord, "and like a hammer that breaks a rock in pieces?– Jer. 23:29

THE MAGNETIC FORCE OF UNITY

Not forsaking the assembling of ourselves together, as the manner of some is; but exhorting one another: and so much the more, as ye see the day approaching. – Heb. 10:25

Yes, you might even have met right at a crusade ground and yet you sometimes find it difficult to go out to programs together. You are sometimes tempted to rather spend that time of gathering alone with your partner. This is where your partner begins to take the place of God in your heart. Do not value the time spent with your beloved more than that spent in the assembly of the righteous.

Another thing that you must learn to do together is also to take active part in the things of God. Join a group in the Church. Be of use to the body of Christ. Do not let your relationship with aman or woman; stop you from being useful to God. Do not however forget to do everything in moderation. Bear in mind that God does not marry. Give to your partner what they deserve in as much as you give also to God. Going to musical programs together as well as other Christian programs serve as a healthy source of entertainment which goes a long way to buildingyour relationship in the faith. It also entrenches the relationship in the house of God and also in the general community. People begin to realise that you two have something in common. You have to pass all these stages which will toughen the relationship in preparation for marriage.

DO NOT KEEP IT A SECRET

When Selgelia and I started our relationship, a man of God who was my mentor asked me to put a stop to it immediately without any tangible reason. Not being convinced, we contacted another man of God who said otherwise. We went ahead with it only to realise that the previous man had his own intentions which were absolutely ungodly. These are some of the many tests that your relationship will have to go through before it qualifies for marriage. It will test your level of maturity and also how prepared you are for the step you are taking.

You will have to let a pastor friend or at least a man of God in your Church know that you are in a relationship with whoever he or she is. The response may be either positive or negative. Whatever you do in the end is very personal and you take the ultimate responsibility. I however see it as beneficial to have a man of God know what is going on in your life. He may help you with resources, counselling and prayer which could go along way to help your young courtship.

Let us not forget to mention other relevant people like your parents, friends and other close relatives who will in no small way influence your relationship. These people can however not impose their opinions on you. Consider their responses as genuine pieces of advice and give them the necessary reaction through prayer and careful consultation. The final decision is however dependent on you because in the long run, it is your life.

Remember also that people give advice based on their own opinions which could be as limited as yours. Some may also be based on a personal bias or interest. Do not let people decide for you when it comes to issues as important as marriage. People may not see what you see. This also does not mean that you should arrogantly brush people aside and follow your heart which may be moving on the fast track of lust. Do not forget that in the multitude of counsel, there is safety.

Where no counsel is, the people fall: but in the multitude of counsellors there is safety. – Prov. 11: 14

One benefit of making your relationship open is that you are protected from deception. I have heard of instances where one man has proposed to three or four women and they are all in a relationship with him without anyone knowing. Such evil men (and I won't be surprised to know women can do so too) often justify their actions by saying they are still not too sure about any of them so they intend to take them all as close to the altar as possible to see who will eventually win. What happens then is that they end up with one winner and three wounded souls. This is not the will of God. If you do not want to end up among the casualties, make your relationship as open as possible.

ASSOCIATIONS

No relationship thrives on its own. We are naturally designed to live and thrive in communities. For this reason, your relationship will also find itself in various forms of communities such as Church, work colleagues, old school friends, social clubs and family groups among others. You have to test the influences which are exerted on your relationship by these groups. Some may bring you closer together, others may cause tension. Some may lead you to achieve great things together whilst others may cause constant arguments. You have to be smart to only expose your relationship to the environments that cause it to thrive, not the ones that kill it.

He that walketh with wise men shall be wise: but a companion of fools shall be destroyed. – Prov. 13:20

Avoid groups where you as a couple or either of you are always talked down. Avoid groups that will introduce you to thoughts that reduce trust or things that destroy the purity of the relationship. Avoid gatherings where alcohol, drugs and other lewd practices occur. Avoid gatherings where the dignity of marriage is undermined.

THE IMPORTANCE OF GRAVITY

My brethren, count it all joy when ye fall into diverse temptations; knowing this, that the trying of your faith worketh patience. But let patience have her perfect work, that ye may be perfect and entire, wanting nothing. – Jam. 1:2-4

You have received approval or otherwise from your pastor, parents and friends. You have made your decision to go ahead. Now is the time of ascension. You have to fasten your seat belt for the take-off. You have to climb in the opposite direction of gravity. If you can pass this final test without giving up, you have what it takes to marry. It takes discipline to marry. You therefore have to pass some disciplinary tests during your courtship to show that you will not abuse your marital rights. It is for this reason that I am telling you to count it all joy when the rough times come during courtship.

Rough times will build you up and give you experience for a successful marriage. You learn discipline and maturity during courtship if you really want to. If you went in just for the fun of it or because people say that you are getting old, then you are in for the mess of your life which will always be part of you. Marriage is not for boys and girls and neither is courtship. It comes with a huge responsibility which even involves human lives. A person can be brought into the world and a person can die as a result of the activities which go on in a relationship. The police are not too far away from a courtship, neither is the doctor. Have you ever heard that a man beat his girlfriend till she died? What about abortion and its related morbidity and mortality. You need discipline in all spheres of your life to run a successful relationship. It does not matter whether you are born again or not. It is interesting to see people who lack discipline, trying to get into relationships with the intension of getting married. You may not be God but you can predict their end. With all respect, if you are going into a relationship because of sex, beauty, money or recognition, think twice; turn around and save your soul. If you are dead serious, I proudly urge you to proceed.

THE DEADLIEST OF THEM ALL

Flee fornication. Every sin that a man doeth is without the body; but he that committeth fornication sinneth against his own body. – 1 Cor. 6:18

This is one sin that is so cruel. It last but a few minutes but the consequences are far too many. Fornication can lead to the contracting of various sexually transmitted diseases including the most dreaded HIV-AIDS. Fornication can also lead to unplanned pregnancies. This is where the problems begin. Conception is one of the three most spiritual phases in a man's life. This is where the breath of God is breathed upon the fusion of the sperm and ovum. These three things, the sperm, the ovum and the breath of God, come together to form the three dimensional human being who is made up of the body, soul and spirit. Conception is a very spiritual point in the lives of all four parties involved. That is God, the mother, the father and the foetus (child).

Three people come together to decide the destiny of another. What a lovely miracle. Would you like to see this miracle happen in a dirty and sinful way? Would you want this to happen when the two of you are in fear, uncertainty and disgrace? Do not force God to breath upon dirt. If He refuses to breath on such a person, the devil will do it and the result could be dangerous. You may end up bringing into the world, an evil person who may cause so much trouble to many. Remember, you are responsible.

The wicked are enstranged from the womb: they go astray as soon as they be born, speaking lies (doing all sorts of evil). Their poison is like the poison of a serpent: they are like the deaf adder that stoppeth her ear; –Ps. 58:3-4

Let us also not forget that once conception has taken place, abortion is out of the question because it is murder irrespective of the excuse you give it. You may only be pardoned if you kill to save another life. That is if the mother's life is in clear and physical danger. If that is the case, a qualified doctor will certify the abortion with the consent of all the relevant people including the law. Uncertified abortions could lead to the death of the mother.

Do you really want to risk the life of the woman you love? It is not worth it. Just wait. If this woman dies as a result of the abortion, you will never forgive yourself. Now how prepared are you to face the law? Can you stand the shame of a policeman arresting you and putting handcuffs onto your hands because you could not control yourself? Can you stand the conditions in the police cells? What about going to prison for manslaughter or murder? Think twice before you act.

These are some of the temptations that are in relationships. Try your best not to fall into this kind of evil but if you should fall into it, put yourself together, stand up fast and start walking again. Confess to a person you can trust; a matured believer will be the best option. I can assure you that this is a sure way of getting healed.

Confess your faults to one another, and pray one for another, that ye may be healed. The effectual fervent prayer of a righteous man availeth much. – Jam. 5:16

If we confess our sins, he is faithful and just to forgive us our sins, and to cleanse us from all unrighteousness. – 1John 1:9

God bless you and keep you from all evil. Do not give the excuse that if you confess your sins to God, you are through with it. Why confess to God when He saw you doing the act? You can only ask for forgiveness from God but confess your sins to one another and be healed. Do not be proud. After all at that moment, you are a poor and helpless sinner. That is why you have done it. You need help. Concealing your sins will kill you and make a mockery of you. Humble yourself and shout it out. If you really want to keep your dignity, stay away from fornication. If not, get ready to disgrace yourself or to be disgraced. Don't let fornication ruin your beautiful love.

SPEAK THE TRUTH

Ye are of your father the devil, and the lusts of your father ye will do. He was a murderer from the beginning, and abode not in the truth, because there was no truth in him. When he speaketh a lie, he speaketh of his own: for he is a liar, and the father of it. – John 8:44

It is my greatest prayer that you do not find the spirit of lies in the person you love, but my deepest prayer is that you do not rather become a liar to your partner. A lie is one simple means through which satan gets hold of relationships. There are so many reasons why we sometimes think that there is nothing wrong with our "white lies". Be warned, there is no middle place in the things of the spirit. You either belong to one side or the other. You are either speaking the truth or you are lying. Lying will take you to hell so watch out!

There are times you want to keep up a good facade before your fiancé. This will mean that you have to change some things to make them seem what they are not. The temptation will be strong, but resist it. It will create a loophole for the devil to enter your relationship anytime he wants to. Always endeavour to speak the truth even if it means disgrace to you. You will end up being vindicated in the end. Do not allow lies to ruin your beautiful love.

"TOM AND JERRY"

What causes fights and quarrels among you? Don't they come from your desires which battle within you? – Jam. 4:1

Arguments come about because people have different opinions about various issues and it takes humility and wisdom to listen to other opinions. Where these virtues are lacking, you are bound to have loads of arguments which will in turn lead to quarrels.

People also quarrel because they may not understand what the other party really means. Thus where there is some form of ambiguity or unclearness in what is being said one may take it in the negative sense.

Quarrels may also come about where the topic being raised coincides with a negative experience which the other party may have had before. This experience could be a terrible childhood incidence, issues relating to one's family, education, health, physique, tribe or finances among others. It could also be relating to some sin the person has committed and is trying to keep hidden. In any of these instances, the person in question may get upset not because what you are saying is evil in itself but because it reminds them of an inner turmoil. Be sensitive and stop when things take this direction.

One very simple reason why we quarrel is also because we find it hard to forgive when we are offended. Keeping offences in your heart never does you any good. I know that by reason, you have every cause to be angry but there is also enough biblical reason why you should forgive and let go. God richly bless you as you try to forgive when it is hardest to do so.

Forbearing one another, and forgiving one another, if any man have a quarrel against any: even as Christ forgave you, so also do ye." "And let the peace of God rule in your hearts, to the which also ye are called in one body; and be ye thankful. – Col. 3:13, 15.

And forgive our debts, as we forgive our debtors. – Matt. 6:12

If you ever want God to forgive your sins, you must forgive others first. The level of your forgiveness will determine God's level of forgiveness towards you. God richly bless you.

Another thing that leads to quarrels is that people cannot keep quiet and listen until you have finished with what you want to say. When everybody wants to talk at the same time, there is bound to be chaos. Let us learn to listen. We may end up learning a new thing that will help us become better partners. Do not allow arguments and quarrels to ruin your lovely relationship.

NO "U" TURN!

For which of you, intending to build a tower, sitteth not down first, and counteth the cost, whether he have sufficient to finish it?
– Luke 14:28

Are you losing it so soon? Don't give up! Hold on!You can make!

Did you really count the cost before starting this journey? Did you satisfy all the necessary conditions before the sufficient conditions? Are you really in love? If any of your answers to these questions is in the negative, you failed right from the beginning. Just back out and ask for forgiveness. And be careful it does not happen again. If on the other hand you are genuinely in love but your love is being tested, please hold on.

Count the cost first. There comes a time in the life of a courtship when either of the party may start losing interest. Things can even be so bad that both of you may want to call it quits. It is very sad but if the love between you is genuine, it will survive the test of time. True love would have counted the cost before commencing. It will survive.

We will briefly discuss some of the things that can easily cause you to lose interest.

Is a *better* option showing up? This is very true in every courtship. You spend time building a strong relationship only to find out that there is another woman or another man who could possibly fit into the picture better than your beloved does. Watch out! It is part of the test. If you manage to give in to that desire, it will follow you for life. You will leave this old one for the new only to realise that there is another one out there who looks better than them too. Hold on. All women are not the same just as all men are not the same. They all have both positive and negative sides. None of them is perfect. No, neither in beauty, nor in character are two women the same. Whichever of them that you will go for, will be outweighed by another whom you will meet the next day. Do you now realise the importance of the discipline that we were talking about earlier on? It only takes discipline to live with one woman all the days of your life, not beauty. It doesn't take money and education to live with a single man as well. It takes discipline! Be sure that you have it before you rush into any mess!

Also, you could be troubled if you realise that another person is trying to snatch your beloved. Don't let this cause you to leave him or her. Stay on and fight for that which is yours. I don't mean that you should go out and create a public scene but stay on your knees and also keep on talking to your partner about it. Be careful not to approach it aggressively since this could cause frustration which will in turn push them away. Continue to reassure them that you are the best option and that you love them more than any other person may do. Let him know that your love is unconditional. Let her know how unfair and unjust it might be if you will have to lose her for whatever reason. However, if after all these, they insist on leaving, let them go. There is a just God up there who puts things right for His children. He will give you a better one. It is my prayer that God sustains you if you have to go through this painful situation. May He keep you and turn your mourning into dancing again.

Has the *situation* changed? A man falls in love with a woman when he is just a teaching assistant in a university. He has not found any job which fits his qualifications. He falls in love with this lady who works in the university's canteen and gives him extra food any time he goes there to eat. They courted for two years before one day the man receives a mail offering him a job as an assistant governor in the central bank. This man has a master's degree but the woman has no degree at all. Should he go ahead and marry her, now that he is rich? Should he leave her for his secretary who looks better and is more educated? Times like these call for discipline.

A girl falls in love with this boy when they were in sixth form. She gets a scholarship to study medicine in the United States immediately after school. This boy can't even gain admission into the university because he has to rewrite some subjects in order to better his grades. Things have changed. What will you advice them to do? It takes discipline to love through thick and thin.

Are you getting too *bitter*? Offences will surely come whenever two people decide to walk together. When these offences come, there is the temptation to forgive but keep records. When the records begin to pile up, they create bitterness. The bitterness then begins to kill the love you have for your partner. Love then begins to turn into hatred. Satan now capitalises on the hatred to do everything possible to ruin the love. Don't forget that he hates it when two people come together to do positive things. Your united prayer alone moves ten thousand of his demons when an individual prayer can only manage a thousand. Beware of him. Don't give him any chance.

Is he not *pulling up*? It took eight years for me to see Selgelia respond positively to something she had done wrong. That is long after we had married. I told her that was a miracle. I never expected it. We come into courtships with various habits that will take God to change. Some of these habits include arguments, some type of dressing, some eating habits, and attitudes toward education, spending and some weird types of friends. Your partner may never be responding to the proper way of doing things but this is where discipline comes in. If you really love them, you will not be quick to leave. Patience will do its work here until you see the desired results.

GOD WILL SEE YOU THROUGH

He that dwelleth in the secret place of the most High shall abide under the shadow of the Almighty. – Ps. 91:1

My heart is absolutely with you even as you plan to take the bold step of courtship that leads to marriage. The true courtship as we have discussed is not for fun. You are not going into it because you want some fun, but you will always be able to create a good one with the help of God and your own determination. Satan will try his best to get you to mess things up. It will be up to you to either allow him or not. Remember however that God is on the alert to do anything for you. He will be quiet till you call on Him. Use all the spiritual resources that Christ has given us through the Holy Spirit. He is your best companion. Prevail in prayer and talk to the situation in all authority.

Let your courtship dwell under the secret place of the most high. Soak it in prayer. The Lord is on your side. Fear not. Trust Him for a successful courtship. He is for you. You will make it. If He did it for us, He will do it for you.

What shall we say then to these things? If God be for us, who can be against us? – Rom. 8:31

You are more than a conqueror. God bless you and keep you till you join us in the fellowship of the married. Amen.

Printed in Dunstable, United Kingdom

83263230R00109